Pits and Pedestals

PITS
AND
PEDESTALS

A Journey towards Self-Respect

Grace Sheppard

DARTON·LONGMAN+TODD

First published in 1995 by
Darton, Longman and Todd Ltd
1 Spencer Court
140–142 Wandsworth High Street
London SW18 4JJ

ISBN 0–232–52004–6

A catalogue record for this book is available
from the British Library

Phototypeset by Intype, London
Printed and bound in Great Britain by
Page Bros, Norwich

To my Mother
for her common sense
and creativity
❧

To my Father
for his sense of fun
and love of journeying
❧

and to Them Both for their constancy
in their love of God, of others and of me.

Contents

Acknowledgements

It is said that writing a book is a lonely business. Writing one on self-esteem has felt dangerous. This particular journey has been an adventure lasting nearly four years. Although at times I have felt alone and at risk of not getting there, it would not have been completed without the good companionship of some special people. They have urged me on. 'You can do it,' must be one of the most energising phrases there is.

First, I thank David, my husband, for his forbearance and his quiet confidence in my work, and for his encouragement and insight. I thank also my sister Evelyn for her engagement with the subject and personal support, and my friends, Pat Starkey, Richard Buck, Hanna McCluskey, Mark Boyling and Godfrey Butland, for being willing to read what I have written and for their helpful honest comments. I am grateful for their time and skills, and for their refusal to doubt that, despite the frustration of many delays, something valuable would be born. I thank Mary Jean Pritchard from Darton, Longman and Todd, who persuaded me to start, and Morag Reeve, her successor as editorial director, for her enthusiasm and her professional and skilled editing.

When I set out to write this book I chose to go to Parcevall Hall, the Bradford Diocesan Retreat House,

Acknowledgements

in the Yorkshire Dales. As I was there for some time, I was invited to join the staff in the kitchen for meals, to give some privacy and continuity from the changing visiting groups to the house. Only they and I know what an intimate and fruitful time that was for all of us. Their day-to-day experience, warts and all, illuminated and validated my ideas. I learned to receive from them without feeling guilty. It was a kind of foot-washing, and God was there. I thank them for their trust, their openness and for their gentle, hidden service. Especially I thank Florence Begley the warden, Lesley Brooker the deputy warden, and Ralph, Carol and John; also Lyn and Heather who have moved on, and the volunteers who slip into the house, unnoticed to guests, to help to cook, to iron, to clean and wash up. If I have learned anything about the sustaining enabling nature of God and the value of affirmation, I learned it there.

Then there is Peter Clare the artist and Carol. Peter's work has inspired me and I am delighted that one of his Stations of the Cross is included in this book, albeit in black and white; they have constantly enquired and encouraged me, and I thank them. I thank also Sirpa Peck, who has kept my shoulder from seizing up after too much writing with a pencil when I was rebelling against word processors, and Margaret Funnell who again generously offered to type the manuscript in all its forms.

Finally I thank the staff at Bishop's Lodge for being who they are and for their personal support, loyalty and interest. Especially I thank Cynthia Miller, George Walker, Kathy Crawford, Tim Stratford and Paul Dawson, all of whom do their hidden and vital work with real humility and grace.

GRACE SHEPPARD
Liverpool 1995

PART I
IDENTITY

Who am I? Who is God?

1
Preparing for the Journey

Is it all right to be me?
Dare I set out to live?

I felt rather a fool. I had been talking with a woman inside her hut in a black township outside Cape Town. During our conversation, I became aware that it had turned quiet outside. I put my head out into the soft warm air to see if the rest of our party was still there. But they had all gone. I froze with disbelief and shock. Indignation and horror threatened to turn to self-pity and panic. I felt abandoned.

Four local men stood outside. Fear and isolation stalked my mind, taunting me with fantasies of being harmed. It was April 1989. The state of Emergency was still in force. It was five months before the publication of my book telling the story of how I conquered twenty-five years of agoraphobia, the fear of public places. Here surely was a supreme test. I did not know where to put myself. If the sandy ground at my feet had opened up and swallowed me I would not have minded.

But there were other feelings too. Something positive stirred. I had been absorbed in admiration for my hostess in her spotless shack, as she helped me to understand how she coped, and I became aware of her courage and resourcefulness. I was astonished at her lack of bitter-

3

ness. Though living in degrading circumstances she had a dignity; she was proud of her home and did not apologise for it. I felt she had accepted the reality of her situation and was truly humble.

On the other hand I realised that my moment had come: my moment to face my own truth and take the opportunity to grow as a person. Should I own up and ask for help, or should I brazen it out as though nothing was amiss?

I did not like what I saw. My prejudiced thoughts of years had set me above this woman and the men outside, and I felt awkward. For I was becoming aware that I was totally dependent on them. I was a guest in their community. Gradually I was being brought down to earth, for we all stood on the same patch of ground.

Several basic questions of identity arose: Who am I? Where am I? What do I want to do? But first I had to deal with prejudices, and to answer some different questions. Did I believe deep down that I was superior to the woman I had just met? Did I really believe that the men I could see were more likely to harm me than they were to help me find my way? It began to dawn on me that those beliefs were not my own. I had imbibed them over the years and then buried them. Now was my chance to get rid of them for ever, and before God I cast them to the sand at my feet, disowning them completely. Immediately I felt free from fear and ready to address the other questions. I stepped down off my pedestal and joined my friends on the ground.

As to my identity, I was no longer clinging to my role as a bishop's wife on an official ecumenical visit. I was plain Grace. It was clear that I was lost and I wanted to find my way back to my party as soon as possible. There was no need to stand on my dignity or assume rank. It would have been ridiculous and might even have been dangerous.

All the negative feelings gave way to a new energy and freedom. I no longer felt abandoned and isolated but among friends. I thanked the woman for talking with me, and moved over to the group of men that a moment ago had terrified me. 'Excuse me,' I said, grinning, 'I'm lost. Could you tell me where my friends went?' using sign language. They understood and grinned in return, which felt like an absolution. I began to see the funny side. They pointed out the direction for me to take and I set off in trust and thankfulness, chuckling inside at the incongruous spectacle of a woman in an off-white Marks and Spencer suit in the middle of Africa, picking her way across the sandy soil between the sea of shacks and having to stop to take directions from people at each new turning.

Twenty minutes later I arrived at the edge of the township and rejoined the party. I had not been alone, for holding my hands were children who had come out of their homes to meet me. To crown my lesson in humility I discovered that no one in my party had missed me!

∾

In that situation I was eventually enabled to own myself as I was. This has often been difficult for me to do, for ever since childhood I have found myself in a dilemma. Being a creative person I enjoy things like painting, singing, gardening and cooking. However, in sharing my enjoyment of these activities I have been confronted with a powerful voice of caution which has prevented me from presenting my efforts with any degree of proper pride or confidence. I have felt driven to curb my straightforward enjoyment for fear of boasting. Like so many I still cannot accept praise simply and graciously.

I well remember an incident at school when I was a teenager. It was time to elect a new school games captain. There was much excitement and discussion in the school about who it would be, and names were being tossed about for days. Mine was among them. There was lobbying which I did half-heartedly, not wanting to push myself unduly. I may have imagined it, but I was led to believe that I was a front-runner and a popular choice. I was good at games, and had captained sides before. I came from a keen sporting family and both my parents had excelled in sport; it was in my blood. Caught up in the excitement of the election, I wanted to be 'it'. I was competing, among others, with a good friend. She was more assertive than I by nature, but we were both fit for the job.

The whole school had gathered in the hall. Girls jostled to find a seat. On the blackboard the nominations were chalked up, including ours. Tension was in the air. Election papers were given out, which we marked with our choice shielding our papers in guarded secrecy. They were collected and counted. Then came the moment for announcing the result, and we held our breath. My friends had assured me that it was a foregone conclusion that I would win. I had no reason to doubt them.

When my friend's name was read out, it crackled like a pistol shot. She had beaten me to the post. Stunned with disbelief, I swallowed back the tears. I looked at my friends and suddenly felt very lonely. Had they betrayed me and changed their minds at the last minute? Had I misunderstood them? Had I misread the signs? Furious questions flew around as I tried to pick myself up. I felt I had nowhere to go. What had happened to me?

I was used to competitive sport and could normally lose graciously. But this was different. Somehow I had set my heart on being chosen and I felt let down. I was disturbed to find that in congratulating my friend, my heart was not in it. I was jealous of her for pushing me off my pedestal. I felt hurt and all at sea. I felt unable to hold my head up. I felt a fool.

And then in private I applied my rather punishing Christianity to what had happened. I blamed myself for being too proud in the arrogant sense. I came to believe that it was my pride that was the problem and needed some attention. The only way I knew was to acknowledge it in my prayers to God, and to seek to change. With a measure of self-disgust I put myself down further without fully understanding what I was doing. My pride, I thought, revolved around the little word 'I', and I studied to remove it.

Each time I used the word 'I', I felt guilty. I attempted to avoid using it in letters and conversation, and I would not talk about myself if I could help it, but directed attention to others. I decided to wear unremarkable clothes, walk at the side of corridors and sit out of the limelight – out of the way. Yet I knew deep down that I was not being myself. It did not feel natural. At home when my mother called me bossy or Miss Know-All, I flew into a hurt rage of rationalisation, as it only underlined my failure at putting myself down. At school, persistent stumbles prevented me from excelling and from enjoying piano and drama performances. Poor handwriting and messy work only showed that my self-confidence was at a low ebb. When my housemistress called me to her room to express her disappointment that I wanted to leave at seventeen I flounced out in frustration, returning almost immediately in a desperate last throw. Putting my head round the door I flung out the words, 'At this rate you're giving me an inferiority complex!'

My tactics clearly were not working. My ego would not lie down. The more I pushed, the more it appeared. One of my favourite choruses was, 'Let the beauty of Jesus be seen in me'. And I would sing it with gusto. It was genuinely what I wanted. But the words 'in me' came to mean 'in spite of me'. And of course in studying to remove the 'I', I became more self-conscious than ever. I did not know what to do with myself.

On my mantelpiece at college I had a postcard with the words, 'Not I but Christ'. But in my heart I wanted affirmation. I little realised then that the sentence of the text was incomplete. It should have read, 'Not I but *Christ in me*, the hope of glory.' That would have made all the difference.

For me the call to humility had become confused with self-denial to the point of annihilation.

Christian people are exhorted to be humble and to give God the glory for work well done, which is where it belongs. I have now come to realise that somewhere between God and my actions, is a person made in God's image and alive in his world. But I still find it difficult to accept praise without feeling that I should immediately and consciously pass it on, as if after the labouring I had nothing to do with the creation. After delivering our daughter, I was congratulated. That was natural, and gave me significance as a mother; I swelled with proper pride and genuine delight. It was also natural for us as parents to thank God then and there for such a gift. Everything was in place.

But at other times I have not been able to accept simple affirmation without turning a spiritual somersault. My confusion has spoiled some relationships and often sullied the possibility of unselfconscious enjoyment. I even tried to persuade David to think again before I accepted his proposal of marriage. I was terrified of not being good enough for him. I had put him on a pedestal while digging a pit for myself in the name of Christianity, for fear of being sentenced to death for the sin of pride. Something was definitely wrong, and I needed some clues to solve my dilemma. Also I knew that I was not alone with this problem.

I was given a clue when Stephen Sykes, now Bishop of Ely and a theologian, came to stay. He had been addressing an ecumenical gathering of clergy in Liverpool on Truth. He and some others were discussing the lectures, and I overheard him saying, 'Humility is facing reality.' That simple phrase rang clear bells with me. It was just what I needed to begin to solve my dilemma. Years later, the phrase still stands up after putting it to the test on many occasions. Learning to face reality at times of success and of failure, means that I can acknowledge my Creator, the source of my life and talents, at the same time as accepting my achievements and my failures as part of me. Then I can go on to be genuinely and properly proud of myself, acknowledging the truth that I am an interdependent being. In the end I have to take responsibility for both my being and my doing while I am on this earth, and to account for it. I will be more effective in that if I am honest about how I feel, and if I am sensitive to other people. I need to be watchful for anything that will cause me to forget or run away from the final authority and source of my life, which is God.

So having been given this clue to dealing with those moments when the balance is at risk, I want to try to share in more detail some of the daily quest to face my own reality. In order to do that I have chosen to offer two opposite poles in each chapter so that from looking at extremes we may find a lively balance, somewhere in the space between them. It will differ for each of us according to our experience. It is important that we make this a personal quest.

Together with a commitment to personal honesty, the other aid or clue to reaching our destination is faith. It is believing that God loves us. Also it is believing that he will not desert us as we travel. Refusal to put those factors in our haversack will have serious consequences. We will need to go on looking for him, especially as we veer towards the extremes that I have mentioned. It is really a question of living more fully within the bounds of being human. I believe we can help one another to a more gradual, but no less real, experience of new life bubbling up within us.

Everything that follows will be considered in the light of my belief that God is a loving God. I believe that unconditional love is at the heart of all that he made, and determines all his actions. His ways with his creation, especially with people, are essentially loving and creative and reflect his respect for our dignity as human beings. He is not a God who shames or embarrasses us, but a Creator who designed us to be fully alive in the ups and downs of human existence. He stepped down to be with us in human form, in the person of Jesus Christ, suffering the greatest indignity of all where even his identity was publicly questioned as he died.

Yet he endured through suffering and through death, to see new life. This made new beginnings possible for every person, for we are all made in his image.

Somewhere in this earthly space between birth and death, lies a place of life and energy where the negative and the positive meet. I only dare to make this journey because I want to discover a greater understanding of true humility, and to distinguish it from the false. I have begun already to discover the freedom that comes from being more truthful under God's love. New energy is being released.

To make this journey together will be much more fun, and much more rewarding than soldiering on alone with our dilemma. So we set out in faith with the aids to our journey, of truthfulness and the fact of God's love. At the end we hope to be spiritually fitter, with backs straighter, necks more flexible, and with heads ready to be held high with proper pride and, at the same time, ready to bow in worship.

2
Significance and Obscurity

Somewhere between significance and obscurity is a place of watchfulness. Here, we can notice whether, like a photograph, we are being over- or under-exposed.

'Paint the shadows and the picture will paint itself.' So said our tutor while on a special-interest painting holiday. He was teaching us the importance of luminosity in painting. Paying attention to the shadows is as important as noticing the direction of light. One without the other is like a photographic negative where reality is reversed. A picture needs both in order to be lively and to reflect the truth. It is the same with us.

Everyone needs to be noticed sometimes. But at other times we may need to slip into the shade to prevent over-exposure. We need to pay some attention to ourselves, as well as to others. In the creation of the world, God provided us with an ideal example by causing the earth to revolve round the sun, so giving everyone a chance of being in the light and also to rest in the night. Too much light, and we shrivel and die. Too much darkness, and we grow pale and lifeless. Creation flourishes when the balance is right.

We are part of creation. Neither the reality of a landscape, nor of a person, is accurately reflected unless the identity of the original is made clear. We need to know what is there in the first place. For ourselves, we need to pay some attention to establishing our own identity.

Once identity is established, day and night, light and shade can come and go. Nothing can shake the fact that an object is still there whatever happens, even if it disappears in a mist. It is so with us. We need to know that we exist before we can be creative.

Like God we need to be able to say, 'I am', as well as saying, 'I do'. And before we can understand the shadows we need to feel we are significant, for without that sense of significance, it is like being in the dark all the time. In order to know our own significance we need to know we are loved unconditionally; only then can we reach out to others without patronising or diminishing them.

Ideally that sense of being significant and of being loved is given at our beginning, in childhood. Later on there needs to be some adjustment in the amount and quality of loving attention we give and receive in order to bring about a creative balance. Sometimes in adulthood we have to do that for ourselves, and sometimes we will need to ask for help. I needed to learn that rather late in life.

I was four years old when World War II was declared. My father was the vicar in his first parish while my mother, who suffered from asthma in the London smogs, ran the ten-bedroomed unheated vicarage. Being the eldest of four children I began life feeling special. Within two years my brother was born and I had to learn to share my limelight with him. As well as an outgoing, carefree personality he had beautiful blond curls. With my straight brown hair I remember feeling jealous of his curls and of the ready attention he received from complete strangers. Sometimes it would feel like being elbowed out of the way or being knocked off a pedestal. Later we both had to make room for our two sisters. We had had our share of the initial limelight. The art for my parents was to enable each of us to learn to be both ordinary and special in their eyes and in our own, and to love and respect each other. Part of what distinguished us from one another was our names.

Naming is part of the natural preparation for a child's arrival into the world. The name we are given distinguishes us from everyone else. It marks our uniqueness and it helps us to know who we are in relation to other people. Eventually it is a name which we take for ourselves. We learn to respond to it, to say it and write it. We attach it to our work and to our communications; our signature is a sign of our being. It gives us an identity of our own and a reason to hold up our heads and meet the rest of the world.

In the Bible God names himself, I AM. There is no mistaking his identity, no apology, no awkwardness. If we are made in his image, then it follows that it is good to know who we are, and to be named.

My name was not given to me without thought. Both my parents are Christians, and the grace of God was and is at the heart of their faith. Unconditional or undeserved love is something they wanted to signify in the name of their first child. I am glad of that.

I treasure an old photograph of my father and mother when they were young parents. In the picture my father is joyfully lifting me as a baby into the air, while my mother looks on with pride and happiness. That photograph helped me, when struggling with a dwindling sense of my own worth some years ago, to recall how much I was loved in my beginning. We all need tangible signs of reassurance like that from time to time. The experience of being loved early on helps us make sense of the two great commandments, to love God and to love our neighbour as ourselves. Putting it into practice is not so easy, and for most people there are setbacks.

Naming alone does not guarantee that we are wanted and loved. There are many who are born to parents and into homes where that sense of being important is absent; they are given shadows instead of limelight. As each of us is born into a state of dependence, with the vulnerability of new-born babies, there is good reason to emphasise the love of God at an early stage of our life as a child. But teaching is not enough. We need to know what it means in our being.

So many of us have become self-conscious and uncomfortable with ourselves and with each other. We have become unsure who we are, and fearful of losing our dignity. We fight for recognition or retreat to a lonely place and wonder what has gone wrong. Instead of sharing our problems openly and naturally with friends, we often allow those problems to build up until they assume chronic proportions. We hide our vulnerability for fear of losing what self-esteem we have left. We cease to trust each other. We wear a mask to hide the part of ourselves we are ashamed of. Often that part has nothing to do with wrongdoing, but more to do with not coping. We begin to hide our humanity.

During the years when I suffered from agoraphobia, I tried to be noticed as a lively fun-loving person, covering up the fear and shame that I felt for not functioning as a fully independent healthy human being. My husband used to be an England cricketer before being ordained as a clergyman. When he became a bishop, that gave me a public role too. Over-conscious of this, I produced a public face and a private one. The public one was serene and smiling, and the private one reflected inner pain and struggle. Deeper still, my emotions churned in me on public occasions like clothes in a washing machine. I did not want people outside my close circle of family and friends to know that I could not go shopping like everyone else, or sit in a theatre, a church or other public place without crippling and debilitating panic overwhelming me. After all, I thought, I had my pride and dignity to preserve. I must not let the side down, rock the boat or draw attention to myself.

So I selected a bright shiny image from my store, in which I appeared totally in control, and I polished up the talents that I could exercise in the safety of my home. Entertaining and homemaking; I had no problems there. At home I was relaxed – until I had to go out. Outside my home I was as tense as an elastic band. Only close friends knew what I was hiding. Others tell me they had no idea about it, but thought I was one of those infuriating people who could always cope with any problem, and they envied me.

Hiding is no answer in the long term, because hiding can prevent us from being truly ourselves. Instead we become divided deep down and are never really sure who we are. Put harshly, we become hypocrites, projecting one image in public and being someone else in private.

What we hide most is our vulnerability. We are fearful of giving too much of ourselves away and shy away from anything to do with weakness. We concentrate on being strong and successful. Anything less, we tell ourselves, is not good enough. And so we set ourselves on the road to the unattainable goal of perfection. When we find ourselves constantly falling short of perfection, we can become depressed and out of touch with human reality. Our self-esteem suffers.

We need to find a way of helping one another to retrieve that sense of personal worth, and of being able to trust one another in our weakness. This would prevent us from living out this side of our humanity in the shadows, separated from the whole. We need to call in question the belief that the most dignified way of being human is to be successful, and to be physically and mentally healthy all the time. This is an image that has been built up over the years, particularly in Western Society, through advertising and other means. In our heart of hearts we know that that image does not reflect real people, yet we dare not challenge it. We fear being labelled naive, idealistic or even boring. Again, we are afraid of rejection. So we need the courage to call some of that bluff and begin to disclose a little more of our own experience with those whom we fear may reject us. We will be surprised by the number of people who come out of their own shadows as a result of our action. It just needs one to start the ball rolling.

It was hard for me to acknowledge that my agoraphobia was not going to disappear by itself or until I decided to do something about it. Although there were slow signs of increased confidence over the years, it was my need to retain some semblance of dignity that prevented me from retreating altogether. Staying in the mainstream of people was important, despite the cost. Being in a relatively public position, there would be questions asked if I disappeared from view. Occasionally I would be described in the Press as 'a private person'. But gradually there were pressures to disclose my position, and the strain of pretending became too great. It is harder to hide when you are in the public eye, and the deception can therefore be greater. But unless we take steps, however small, we remain in a kind of prison for ever.

In prison, if there is a danger that a prisoner should escape, there is greater watchfulness from the prison staff and the barricades are made stronger. In my prison, my barricades were my home. I made it comfortable and dreaded leaving it. At home where I was both loved and needed, I felt that I mattered. But outside I was not so sure. Trusting other people became difficult. I was afraid they would reject or betray me if I did not measure up to their expectations. From somewhere I had gleaned that being myself would not be good enough in the world at large. I was my own prison officer. Occasionally I let my prisoner out for walks, but never alone, afraid of something escaping that could not be controlled. That something was my creative self. Only when it dawned on me that the life I was controlling needed to be released did I discover that I was the prisoner and that underneath it all I wanted to live. I had the power to sack the prison officer and release myself. I had the key, but I needed help to turn it. I needed a lot of reassurance that I would survive the escape.

Years ago, realising that I needed help I joined the throng of people just below the surface of our society, and sought the services of a clinical psychologist. It was not easy making regular visits to her as it meant travelling a distance alone and by train. Also there were natural enquiries about where I was off to. Venturing out on my own felt unsafe at first, and I did not trust many people to hold my secret with the discretion I felt it warranted.

Learning to control my life outside the prison meant letting it out little by little. Like the Beirut hostages, Brian Keenan, John McCarthy and Terry Waite, after their homecoming, I needed some time and space to 'debrief'. I was not ready to submit myself to the curiosity of some whom I felt would not understand or keep my confidence. I was afraid of harsh criticism and of my story travelling into the Press before I felt ready to stand up for myself.

But underneath it all I wanted to bring about change. I wanted to be free, whatever it cost me. So I chose some obscurity in which to work. In a private consulting room, and in my own home, I began to regain a sense of my own worth and significance. I knew what I wanted. I wanted to live again in the open with nothing to hide. I wanted the strength to own my vulnerability as being both acceptable and part of me. In fact I was climbing down from the dizzy heights of trying to be perfect. I was rejoining the human race.

The more I discovered my own strengths, the less fearful I became. The more important I was enabled to feel, the less I reached for my defences and weapons. It touched me deeply to find that my therapist had remembered what I had said the previous week, and based her questions on what had happened to me since the last session. Whether she made notes or not was beside the point. She showed interest which felt genuine. Her skill and sincerity found a way through my scepticism. I felt she enjoyed my company. She retained a detachment of role that I learned to value till the distance became a space in which to breathe and to make my own decisions.

The culmination came when I told her that I had been asked to write a book. I half expected a guarded response. Instead she jumped in her chair with eyes dancing and said, 'How fantastic!' 'Do you mean you think I could do it?' I said. 'Of course you can,' she replied. The words, 'You can do it,' have released many of us into feeling significant again, and not just in terms of what we can achieve. For our actions arise out of our being; they are inseparable. It is the balance between being and doing that we continually seek.

If our actions arise out of who we are, then we need not be afraid to acknowledge our origins. We can safely consider our identity, which begins as soon as we are born and named. Once we have come to terms with the love and attention, or lack of it, that we experienced in our childhood, this honest reflection will lead us to want to play a part in redressing the balance for others. We will recognise the signs of the kind of imprisonment I have described and want to pay more attention to those who need and want our friendship and service. We will become specially aware of children and those adults who apologise for being who they are.

It disturbs me if, when saying 'Hello' to someone and asking their name, they say, for example, 'Oh! I'm sorry. I didn't realise who you were. I'm Harry Roberts' wife.' This response does not tell me her name but only who she feels she belongs to, and that she feels guilty for being herself. I am disturbed because it is not far removed from my reply to similar questions years ago. 'I'm the bishop's wife,' I would say, and immediately feel awkward. I had offered a clue to my identity but for some reason did not feel my own was good enough. Inside I would be feeling, 'They won't know me. They probably won't want to know me. So I'll give them something that will interest them.' It was a form of name-dropping. Linking myself to my husband in that way made me feel significant. But it did nothing to help me grow up and be myself. It made me blush when someone asked further, 'Yes, but who are you, and what do you do?' I have had to learn to rise up and meet that question with the simple truth, whether it interests them or not. In the end it is much more comfortable for all concerned, for then no one is pretending, or apologising; we are simply being. I have often found that beneath the apologising exterior is an interesting and gifted person who has been living in the shadows, or in prison, for too long.

One of the signs of not feeling significant is to show off or make an exhibition of ourselves. We see this in children, but also in some adults. Someone working in a psychiatric unit in a children's hospital told me that she loved working there because she saw children walking with their heads held high after showing signs of disturbance. At first one child would be curled up in a corner, while another would fling a desk across the room, but after they had received some sustained and loving attention and appropriate treatment she could witness some of their balance and self-worth restored.

In his book, *Life after Life*, Tony Parker records the accounts of twelve people who have been sentenced to life imprisonment for murder. All twelve spoke of a feeling of not mattering to their parents as small children. One went on to speak of his experience in prison: 'The thing I was most conscious of was that I wasn't conscious of being anybody. I'd had several months in custody waiting to be tried; nobody had written or been to see me. So far as I could tell nobody knew me or wanted to know me.'

Of course, this feeling of insignificance does not mean that we all become murderers, but it does mean that we are more likely to diminish others to compensate for our own lack of self-worth. Too much time in obscurity is like depriving a plant of light; in the end it ceases to grow or be creative. Facts like these can warn us of the dangers in neglecting our children. Christ had strong words to say to those who offend against children, by sins of omission as much as by commission. 'It were better that a millstone were put around his neck than to offend one of these little ones.' He loved and supported children, giving them a central place in his teaching.

Children need proper care and attention, and so do adults. We can care for one another. We all need to feel valued in our own right; sharing someone else's limelight is not enough. For instance, being engaged and then married to a well known person made me feel extra important for a while. My name and photo appeared in several papers, and I was asked to comment on various subjects to journalists. My friends were interested in whom I was marrying, and the general public was curious about whom David was marrying. But it soon became clear to me that the interest of press and public in me was shortlived, and I became a stepping stone for many to enquire about my husband. At first this seemed natural, but in time I felt used and by-passed. Once again I felt I wasn't good enough. I was not able, then, to see the reality that my husband was more important to the general public, and that it was unreasonable to expect anyone to regard me in the same way. Such was my arrogance. Such was my need.

Humility is facing reality. I have at last found the freedom to accept that while being married gives me the right and privilege to share my husband's life, and he mine, I have no right to expect the same level of public attention, or to scoop his limelight, nor he mine. I have to find a patch of my own in which to experience my worth as a human being. That does not necessarily mean being famous or public. I must do my own living, and not cash in on my husband's experience. We need to leave each other enough space in which to grow as individuals. We need to be watchful for the times when we think we are more important than we really are. We need to respect each other's ground, and make sure our feet are firmly planted on the patch for which we are initially responsible.

It was because of being in the public eye for so long that David and I chose to withdraw to an obscure location for a sabbatical study leave. There we were able to retrieve the feeling of being ordinary again. We withdrew from the place where we were made to feel extra important, because of the role, to a remote highland cottage where the local villagers expected nothing from us except friendliness and the normal respect due from outsiders. They gave us a more intimate sense of belonging and we scaled ourselves down.

Here among the majestic Scottish hills, we discovered new aspects of life that have helped us to see things more in proportion. We saw clearly how privileged we were, and how well served by a loyal staff. We became more keenly aware of the scale of responsibilities that we both carry. This experience enabled us to see one another in a new light where we discovered a new closeness, and also a new detachment. We gave each other space in which to work separately, and we served each other domestically on alternative days.

This time away was not an end in itself, but in order to return as refreshed people. It gave us a sense of the importance of a rhythm in our lives, and a new determination to find one which ensured that we did not become too rigid or defensive in our thinking and actions. Removing ourselves from the limelight had its risks, but we were rewarded with new energy from the change, and we emerged with new insights and horizons. We were cut down to size, yet did not feel diminished. Rather, we felt enlarged and liberated in our spirits.

The effect has been lasting. It has been important to experience a rhythm, an ebbing and flowing of being which helps us to stand back and take another view from time to time.

∾

At the beginning of this chapter we thought about the importance of establishing our identity. This is why Christians look at the life of Christ for a clue to the nature of God and his pattern for their lives. The picture of Christ clearly shows us someone who knew who he was and where he came from. He had a purpose in life which he pursued. He practised finding a rhythm of living which included withdrawing from being the focus of attention from time to time. He noticed those who lived in the shadows, like the poor, the sick, the outcast and the bereaved. He had a special interest in the wellbeing of children. He was angry with hypocrites, especially if they were religious. He was always aware of a higher authority. He loved to the point of death. He is the best model we have for a person of true humility, for he was not afraid of the truth.

3
Success and Failure

Somewhere between success and failure is a place of endeavour. Trying to do things risks embarrassment and failure, but it also enables us to move out of a world of fantasy into the world of reality.

Soon after we arrived in Liverpool I heard that a '*Messiah* for All' was to be performed in the parish church. Donald Gray, the rector, knew of my interest in music and invited me along to join in.

I hadn't sung in the *Messiah* for many years, and greatly looked forward to sharing the experience with other people from Liverpool. I knew it well, and as children my brother and I enjoyed singing in the arias 'He shall feed his flock' and 'Come unto me' together. I believe we sang them well. Also I had specialised in singing at college, but it was many years since school and college performances.

I joined the crowd in the church, and the solo parts were allocated to various plucky volunteers. But there was no one to sing, 'He shall feed his flock' and 'Come unto me'. My pulse began to race. I wanted to sing them. But I had not practised for many years, and I was very nervous, and new to the city.

Eventually, with a little gentle persuasion from a friend who was there and who had accompanied me privately on the piano when we were in south London, I could hold my excitement no longer and agreed to try the solo part.

Although I started all right, it soon became painfully obvious to me that the voice of my fantasies was not the voice of reality. My breathlessness made me unable to sustain the tone or reach the very high notes adequately. So with some embarrassment, and flushed from pumping adrenalin, I withdrew and sat down. I had tried – and failed.

It is important to try. Trying to do things risks embarrassment and failure, but it also enables us to move out of a world of fantasy and into a world of reality. Failing and feeling foolish is something we all experience from time to time but, unless we try, we will not grow, or move from a place of safety where we become locked in, and where eventually we take no risks at all. That place can be dark and lifeless. Eventually we become unwilling, and then unable, to be enlightened with anything new. Sometimes we need to turn our dreaming into doing. Then we can discover the extent of our capabilities and the truth about our talents. We will not know until we try. At least I know now that my voice is for home performances only. By facing something of my own reality, I was humbled.

Being humbled like that freed me to enter a world more suited to the voice I possessed, a world where I could develop it without over-reaching myself, and where the enjoyment – and enthusiasm – could be sustained as well. That is why I joined the Cathedral Singers.

∾

Trying is natural, like a child learning to walk. We make an attempt, or are curious, because we want to see, or discover something. I can recall shrieks of joy surrounding the first steps taken by children of friends, sometimes so sudden that the child nearly lost his balance.

As a mother I remember the deep sense of delight when our own daughter began to walk. I can also remember the intense expression of concentration on her face as she kept going, her eyes fixed on the way ahead. Arriving, she relaxed into our arms wreathed in smiles. She was proud of herself. Then she would try again.

No one would call that arrogance. Unaffected delight in simple achievement is what a child learning to walk can offer us. As parents we were pleased to see her both attempting and achieving something she wanted to do, and we shared her delight.

Yet early on in the life of a child comes a self-consciousness that begins to change that freedom and openness to something more guarded and competitive. That self-consciousness comes through relating to another person. A brother or sister, or two children at school, work side by side and they begin to compare each other's efforts. A younger child, inspired by an older one, will try to do as well and, finding he cannot, becomes frustrated. The feeling of being better or worse than another person begins to grow. In school, children begin shielding their work from each other as though they had produced something they were ashamed of or that would be taken away from them in some way. The teacher comes round to comment. Quite soon, work is displayed for all to see.

Learning to receive criticism is part of growing up. Constructive criticism, sensitively offered, helps to train and guide. Destructive criticism can be devastating in its effects. For example, we knew a man who grew up in inner-city Glasgow and was a very gifted youth leader. When George Burton was a teenager he fell in love with a girl of the same age. He was uncertain whether she would accept him, so he wrote to her, declaring his love. She replied, rejecting his love, and returned his letter with all the mistakes in grammar and spelling corrected in red.

The shock was so great that for over forty years he did not write another word except his name. He became so ashamed of being unable to write, that he swore to secrecy the few he entrusted with his secret. Those few did not betray his trust. Eventually, after all those years and after much mental anguish, he wrote a book in his own hand, called *People Matter More Than Things*.

As children we begin to build barricades to shield us from hurt and harm and from destructive criticism. So we begin to cling to what we know and possess, while at the same time we long to be 'grown up' and 'getting on' like the older ones. We begin to see ourselves in relation to other children, as well as to the adults who care for and teach us. We find ourselves looking up to people.

It is here that it is important that children receive affirmation of who they are, and encouragement and praise for their efforts. This reinforces their sense of mattering at a time when it is becoming clear that others matter too. Without that reinforcement the balance of mattering is tipped, and a child may begin to feel that he has been cast aside in favour of someone else. This is also a time when the seeds of an inner authority are either nurtured or neglected. The sense of being good enough, or all right, begins very early and needs attention to thrive. If we are afraid of 'spoiling' our children, we can bear in mind that there will probably be plenty of knocks later on to curb their ego.

The sense of mattering that I am referring to is close to the will to live. Wanting to live is different from wanting to achieve or succeed. It is wanting to *be*, and to go on being, that I am talking about.

Where schools introduce lists involving the placing

of children at the top and also at the bottom of a list, they reinforce a set of values about being successful. When I was at school we all crowded round the notice board for the lists of results after examinations. Those lists excited me – when I was doing well. For ordinary tests and examinations our names were placed in order of achievement. There was a line drawn to indicate those who fell above and below the pass mark. If your name appeared below, then you knew you had failed.

I can remember the thrill of being top. I can also remember the thud inside the pit of my stomach of finding my name near the bottom. Fortunately for me that did not happen very often, but for some girls it did. So those girls grew up believing they were 'not very bright', while the rest of us grew up believing we were brighter than they were. So at work we were divided; at play on the sports field the divisions were different. Socially we crossed those boundaries sometimes, but we mostly stayed with people of similar ability. Even so, the belief that we were brighter intellectually than others became confused with the belief that we were better people. Brighter meant better. So academic and sporting achievement carried more value than whether or not a person was a good and loving human being.

The incentive in that system to do well was fine so long as you were clever or good at sport. Some names usually appeared at the top. Others usually appeared at the bottom, and all were publicly displayed. Appearing at the top or bottom said nothing about effort. Mostly effort was not rewarded; it was success and achievement that counted.

One day years later my daughter came home with the news that she and two of her friends, who were due to move to secondary level, had made the grade to go to grammar school. But there were only two places.

The girl who had 'failed' to be given a place was one of the most sensitive, caring eleven-year-olds I had ever met. She had a natural dignity. She also struck me as being an intelligent person, and was certainly a full and equally valued member of their group. The fact that they would be separated from each other as they continued their education put burdens on all the members of that group. I was struck by the sense of natural justice that burned in those young lives, and by their sense of outrage that, as school-mates, something had drawn a line between them and between their continuing to learn together. The experience drew indignation from the children and may have contributed to destructive attitudes towards authority in the future. No one will know what happened to the girl in her heart when she heard the result and how it affected her sense of dignity and self-esteem.

I cannot agree with those who say 'That's life,' as if that meant it is how life should be. Adults who have grown up in a competitive world perpetuate a way of looking at life which implies that some people are 'better' than others because of what they 'do'. So we find that we judge one another by actions and performance rather than accepting one another's diversity. We call that 'the real world'.

Unless we are always top in the lists, as adults we become less self-confident, and look round for reassurance that we are still in the running – still part of the whole, and not too different. We become slaves of fashion or victims of others' approval. We begin to apologise for not being good enough or clever enough or acceptable in any sense. And we begin to lose that inner dignity of an unspoilt child who is always pleased with himself for trying.

I began to wonder where I had picked up the strong

sense of not being 'good enough' which followed me into my adult life. This was in spite of being, in fact, 'good enough' at most things at school, being loved by my parents, achieving entry to a prestigious teacher training college, and becoming its senior student. Socially I was middle class, and marrying an England cricketer gave me further credibility. When my husband became a bishop that sense of counting in society increased even more along with the expectations. Everything was going for me according to one set of values.

But there was another set of values at work. I believe that this was due to a confused picture of God that I had developed. From somewhere I came to believe that I was not good enough for God. On the one hand I knew he loved me and that there was nothing for me to do to earn my salvation, for Christ had paid that price on the Cross. On the other, I was terrified that in the final analysis I would be judged unworthy and eventually be cast away. For some reason I felt unable to be completely myself. I dreaded Judgment Day, for I felt my account of myself would be inadequate, and so I would be ultimately rejected. There was a curious unidentified and pervading guilt that I could not explain. And I know I am not alone in that.

I think that it may have been because, as a very young girl, I came to believe that if Christ died for my sins, then I was responsible for his death on the cross. But I did not know what those sins were. Did it mean that every time I disobeyed my mother I crucified Christ? Did it mean that every time I shouted at my brother I crucified Christ? But then I was not a very disobedient child, and my brother and I quite liked each other despite my jealousy of his blond curls! There was a thread of feeling that I would never be good enough which wound its way into my adult life. I was both good and bad. I felt both loved and likely to be rejected at the same time. It was as though my father would come in to kiss me goodnight, telling me he loved me, and in the morning had gone without leaving word. Although as far as I can remember he never did that, he did have to go away during the Second World War, and there may have been some untidy threads around his leaving that were never resolved.

So, when we face failure, it makes a difference if underneath it all we know we are all right, acceptable and good enough. Deep down we need to find a place where we go on approving of ourselves through failure and believing that God goes on accepting us despite, for instance, not being recommended for a job, or failing exams, or having a breakdown in health or relationships. It is an added bonus if we have someone else who believes in us too. We need to know that failing is not a punishment or a sign of disapproval. Failing is failing. Somehow we need to find a way of facing failure as a fact, without allowing a sense of not being good enough to add insult to injury and cause us to hang our heads in shame.

Although failure can be a fact, it can also be a feeling. I know about that feeling of failure. Having a breakdown, as we call it, and agreeing to enter a psychiatric clinic for psychotherapy thirty-eight years ago felt like a massive failure. I was young and newly married, and had been full of high hopes.

Feelings of failure lead to our becoming more affected by what others think, and we begin to lose a sense of our own authority. In our confusion we begin to revert to looking for a parental-type authority in others of our own age and those in positions of institutional authority. And we begin to blame. Bishops and managing directors, headteachers and politicians become objects of either praise or blame. They become our new parents, and we revert to being children who cannot grow up, and who are dependent on their guidance and affirmation for our survival. Similarly, we metaphorically kick them in the shins when we are frustrated.

Good parenting and good teaching enable a child to retain a belief in his own ability to distinguish between what is acceptable to himself and what is not. That is when standards of both behaviour and performance begin to be formed. If this process works then we will grow up to know how to assess ourselves objectively, how to be pleased with ourselves and then how to enjoy ourselves. This process includes our achievements and successes. It will not lessen our enjoyment in the creative process, for we will want to go on taking part in it, without fearing that our enjoyment may be taken for arrogance by others, making us feel judged and rejected by them. We can hold our heads up with proper pride, and with dignity. Like a child learning to walk, we can express genuine delight.

We read in the Bible that when God created the world, he stood back and surveyed his work, and found that it was good. Also he looked on Jesus at his baptism, and said, 'This is my Son in whom I am well pleased.' Something has gone wrong if we cannot genuinely enjoy our own creations with unaffected joy like a child. Instead of relying on the tick on the page of an exercise book to feel good, we can first tick our own work and then prepare ourselves for assessment by another.

Like children, we all progress at different paces. Our levels of concentration and determination vary. Depending on the task in hand we also need inspiration and a sense of direction, and we all need encouragement – without that we begin to lose heart. With encouragement, there is no telling where we shall end. The sky's the limit!

As a musical child I received a great deal of inspiration from my parents. There was music in our home. My father's bass-baritone voice gave us all pleasure, and we were proud of him when he sang the solo parts in amateur performances of oratorios. My mother was musical; she played the piano well and we would beseech her to continue. Also we had a pianola and enjoyed fooling our guests with vigorous performances of Chopin and Rachmaninov from an adjoining room.

Consequently we grew up with a love of singing and piano-playing. My brother and I would sing together as two treble voices, imagining we would become another Isobel Baillie and Ernest Lough. The thrill of singing together coupled with parental pride when we sang Mendelssohn's 'I waited for the Lord' is still with us. I think that was when I first experienced 'a buzz' in performing in front of people. It was at home that I first tasted the rewards of trying.

But above all it was attempting something together that kept the spirit of life and creativity alive. My parents' enthusiasm and skill inspired us. Their delight in sharing that with us made us want to participate. When one of them sat at the piano, one of us would often try to push in, itching to have a go ourselves. The motivation was strong.

Then learning to play an instrument at school helped us to realise that effort was needed to improve. There was 'piano practice' on the timetable and later on, 'choir'. I was fortunate to attend a school where music was a high priority. We were encouraged at all levels and I enjoyed practising. The motivation continued rising, and was particularly helped by the two music staff members.

They were totally unalike, both in character and in appearance. Miss Greatorex, my piano teacher, was large and short-sighted and she loved her instrument. Miss Melhuish, also bespectacled, was petite and very precise, and knew what she wanted to achieve. Her subject was musical appreciation and she certainly succeeded in enthusing us. Both women clearly enjoyed working together, and their personalities shone through without pretence. They communicated their enthusiasm to us in quite different ways, yet remained open to the inevitable surprises of working with a group of lively girls.

Striving to be good, or even the best, was helped by Miss Greatorex and her sense of fun. One day when the whole school was waiting longer than usual for prayers to begin in the Hall – a serious business – Miss Greatorex was playing a hymn as a voluntary. Then I caught sight of her looking sideways through her thick glasses with a hint of mischief in her eye as she began to jazz up the hymn tune a little and was looking to see if anyone noticed. This relaxed the tension, without distracting from the reverence. I am afraid that someone may have 'had a word' with her, as I do not remember it happening again. Her lightness became confined to private piano lessons.

Though recognising that there are proper times and places for that kind of playing, I think we were the poorer when she stopped. Her jaunty spirit relieved the intensity that often accompanies serious study and certain kinds of religion, and her example helped to reinforce an attitude that I grew up with, that it is all right to relax during times of serious learning. In fact I believe it is essential.

∾

A relaxed attitude can and should, I believe, extend to

competition. Competition is not wrong in itself, but an unbroken atmosphere of competing exhausts and divides people. We need respite and time to stop and reflect, so that we can see more clearly what we are doing to one another. To avoid relentless and unbridled behaviour, competition needs to be interrupted.

The trouble with success is that it is hard to sustain. If we become used to it, it can go to our heads so that we expect to be top all the time. When something happens to knock us off our pedestals we search for something or someone to blame, as if it should not have happened. Instead of giving the other person an experience of being first for a change, we cling to our position, fighting off any would-be contenders in desperate and sometimes ridiculous ways. We put them down so that we may enjoy the feeling of being 'up'. We find ourselves trying to reduce another person's standing. But this arises out of an inability to face our own reality in relation to others. So we can become jealous and cling to our position.

From knocking down another's sandcastles on the beach as children, or houses made of building bricks in the play-pen, we can become adults who are in danger of destroying another person's reputation or livelihood. Whether it be their character or their business, we can do this in arrogant self-defence and sometimes in the name of competition. We become domineering, bossy individuals who gradually cease to care about other people, and guard our own castles at all costs against the possible destruction by others.

Such behaviour arises out of fear of failure, and in that vulnerable place there needs to be someone there helping us to face reality, encouraging us and reassuring us that there is life beyond our original dreams of success, and that it is still possible to hold up our heads without blaming or hurting others and without bearing down on ourselves. We need to be helped to see the funny side as well, to save us from leaping on to our high horses and galloping into a fantasy land where, in our self-deception, we see everyone else being at fault.

Life is not meant to be a competition. We should be living because we want to, from within, and not because we are driven from without. We should be caring because we have been cared for and want to pass that caring on to others. We should be succeeding because we are enjoying what we do, not simply as a response to gratify those who think we need an incentive.

It is not too late to change our course. Sitting comfortably in an armchair blaming the government, our parents or simply 'them', when things go wrong for us, is not the way to freedom and dignity and new life. There is something we can do. We can get back in touch with our will to live and try to see what it is we really want to do. I have heard it said, 'If at first you don't succeed, ask yourself why.' Learning from our experience, we can re-set our sights, chuckle a little at our own humanness, and remember we are not alone. Then we can stand up and start again.

4
Self-Neglect and
Self-Indulgence

Somewhere between self-neglect and self-
indulgence is a place for self-respect that is neither
arrogant nor humiliating, but energising,
liberating and where we can be truly ourselves.

When I meet someone from the train for the first time,
to enable our visitor to pick me out in the crowd I
sometimes describe what I look like. I could say, 'I am
tall and fair, about 5'8", with short mouse-coloured hair,
and I shall be wearing a navy jacket.' I could describe
myself in another way, 'I am the eldest of four children,
my father is a retired priest and my mother was a
teacher. I am married to a bishop, and am mother to one
daughter.' Or I could say to our visitor, 'This morning I
wrote ten letters, made up your bed, picked flowers for
your room, and put finishing touches to a script I am
writing.' I could also say, 'I am made in the image of
God, just like you.' All these things are true. We are a
mixture of things. We are what we appear, and what
others have made us. We are what we do and we are
what we are: that is, creatures of God, and objects of
his love.

'Be yourself,' we say to one another, 'Be that person
and do not try to be anyone else.' But that is not always
as simple as it appears. 'Look after yourself,' 'Take care
of yourself,' we say. But what do we mean? What is it
that needs looking after or caring for? What is this
thing we call self? It is close to that essential dignity

that every person is born with. It is that which keeps us going physically, emotionally, spiritually and socially. It needs attention, because it is precious and something to be proud of. It is easily damaged and obscured, yet it will not lie down. It is the spirit of life.

It is easy enough to tell someone else to be themselves, but not so straightforward to attend to our own integrity. Nowadays it has become fashionable to attend courses on self-esteem. Self-esteem is under threat, and people need guidance to maintain or regain their self-respect. There are long waiting lists for counselling services and for psychotherapy, and there is much discussion about alternative medicine and holistic approaches to healing.

We are confronted on our television screens and in the newspapers by pictures of human beings in different parts of the world with very little left but their own starving bodies and scraps of clothing. This affront to their dignity is also an affront to our own, for they are part of us. Yet so often we see springing out of a starving person a dignity which puts us to shame. A crippled and starving mother, still suckling her baby, holds her head high.

When I was in South Africa in 1989, I met women and men whose homes were shacks made of bits of wood and black plastic, and yet who had a dignity about their bearing and in their conversation that shamed me. It also inspired me. There was no self-pity in most of the people I met, but there was unmistakable life coursing through their veins despite their wretched living conditions. Many of us know people who have lost their health, and yet something else has taken over, and radiance transfigures their faces and demeanour. There is a spark that we can all recognise.

We become most truly ourselves when we are stripped

to the bone of our being. We can no longer pretend to be well when we are very ill. We can no longer pretend to be whole when we are broken. But when we are stripped to the bone like that, we need other people to affirm and support us.

Being isolated at those times of stripping is abandonment of the deepest kind. It damages the dignity of those who are left alone and hardens the hearts of the ones who turn their backs and refuse to come near. When I was in hospital years ago, suffering from cancer, it was wonderful to receive the cards and flowers and messages from those who knew of my situation. That kind of noticing helped me to feel better in myself, and more motivated to take my part in the healing process and face the radiotherapy that was being prescribed. There were others who did not receive that kind of attention, and had to face the cobalt machine alone. Feeling better is an important ingredient in becoming whole. We can help one another to be healed.

Most of the time, we in the Western world are relatively fit, have enough money to live on, a job and a roof over our heads. It is when something happens suddenly to remove those advantages that we are brought face-to-face with our real selves. The clutter falls away and we then discover what we are made of, and who we really are. But most of the time we seek ways of being ourselves without sudden disasters to test us. Many of us have the power to choose how we live and how we look after ourselves, while many others have had that choice removed. We need to make the right choices. We have the whole spectrum from self-indulgence on the one hand to self-neglect on the other. Somewhere in between those polarities lies a place of self-respect that is neither arrogant nor humiliating, but energising and liberating and where we are truly ourselves.

When looking at the extremes of self-indulgence and self-neglect, many questions arise, particularly for religious people. Is not this attending to ourselves selfish? Is not this looking at self one big excuse to indulge in navel-gazing, when it is God who should be receiving our attention? Is it not unhealthy to spend all this time and energy on ourselves, when our time would be better spent attending to others in need? These questions are real and I have both asked them of myself and heard others posing them. Preoccupation with self is selfishness. There are no two ways about it. But some measure of attention to ourselves is necessary if we are to understand anything of the second of the two commandments that Christ left us. He said that as well as loving God, we were to love our neighbours *as ourselves*. Martin Buber, a famous theologian, puts it like this;

They are happy who are at peace with oneself.
To begin with oneself, but not to end with oneself;
To start from oneself, but not to aim at oneself;
To comprehend oneself, but not to be preoccupied with oneself.

As an agoraphobic I was not at peace with myself. I felt that I was not good enough for God or for others. I saw God primarily as a judge rather than as someone who loves me and does not want to humiliate. Discovering fresh truth about God has been good news indeed for me. It has meant taking action to affirm myself at a deep level, because God affirmed me from the beginning. At first this led me to feel selfish. I had to find courage to introduce myself and to step out and be myself when meeting people socially – for example, telling stories at dinner parties which involved my own experience. Even taking trouble over my appearance felt dangerous, for I remembered terrible warnings from Christian speakers in the past, of the perils of spending more time at our dressing tables than on our knees. Presenting myself felt like pushing myself. Speaking with confidence felt like shouting. Speaking clearly felt false. But the reaction was remarkable. Instead of being a person who stood quietly by, smiling passively, I found people wanting to engage in conversation. I rejoined the world of people.

Some people have deep anxieties about the recent trend for engaging in a spirituality which emphasises the gifts and preferences of individuals and how they interact in groups. They say it is too self-centred, and so they give it a wide berth, remain suspicious and condemn those who do take part. 'We should be thinking about God', they say, 'and not about ourselves.' This is partly true, but only partly, and needs challenging.

Loving our neighbours as ourselves implies that a measure of self-knowledge and self-awareness is necessary if we are to engage in loving others as we are commanded. God did not create us in order that we may apologise for who we are, or even pretend we are not really there at all. Christ's personality was strong, and was marked by the actions of a most self-possessed person. These actions included throwing the money-changers out of the temple. 'My house is called a house of prayer, but you have made it into a den of thieves.' He knew when to assert himself and when to withdraw. He went to the hills to be alone with his Father, and alone with himself with only wild beasts and angels for company.

∾

When I was a growing teenager, opinionated and sometimes bossy, my mother would remind me that I was 'not the only pebble on the beach'. That no doubt was an important reminder. But, a little later on, I believe I took that motherly remark too far, until I began to feel that there was something wrong in being a pebble at all. I began to tackle my pride by detaching from myself altogether.

This self-abnegation gave rise to attitudes towards other people – the other pebbles on the beach. I began to notice their strong identities, and compared them with my own. I noticed their expressed wills and wishes, and resented and judged them to be arrogant and self-centred. I began to want them to be like me, working at my act of disappearance and becoming invisible. Stirrings of jealousy would arise when others achieved anything receiving praise. My heart would cry out inside, 'No it's not you, it is God's achievement anyway.' However, what my heart was really saying of others was, 'No don't be yourself because it shows me up. I've decided to be partly me, and when you act like that it reminds me of what I have chosen to neglect, and makes me feel split inside.'

As I mentioned in a previous chapter, there was a time when I believed that anything to do with 'I' was wrong and was to be firmly put in its place. That place was out of sight and out of mind. I have since been asking the question that inevitably arises, 'If God is not in me then where can I find him?' and, 'If God is not in this part of his creation, the human being, even in a small part of us, then why was humanity – his primary joy – such a disaster?' The last question points straight to the story of the Garden of Eden where man and woman were banished from God's presence for disobedience and, I believe, because of arrogant pride.

Instead of believing and trusting God, they indulged themselves and chose to override his direction in favour of their own. They separated themselves from God and organised their own isolation. In effect they banished themselves. And so the rest of us followed suit. In different degrees we became arrogant, sinful human beings, preferring to set our own rules.

The idea that God made us and then, through Adam and Eve's act of disobedience, he rejected us and then ejected us from his nearer presence for ever, makes no sense to me. That Christ was sent such a long time later to both atone for our disobedience, and also to invite us back to God, should we choose to return, is certainly a sign of love and forgiveness. But where was God in the interim period? Was his spirit not with the rejected ones as they wandered and worked outside the garden? Was his stamp not imprinted on them still? Whether original sin or original blessing, I am convinced that God's spirit was not withdrawn from the face of the earth that he created. He lived on somewhere in the heart of humanity despite their rejection of their Maker. Man and woman still mattered to him. He still loved them, indeed he longed for them so much that he sent himself in the person of Christ to settle the score of all disobedience, all arrogance, for all time.

So, when Christ issued the two new commandments, he replaced the old, negative 'Thou shalt nots' with positive things to do. 'Love God, and love your neighbour as yourself,' he said. 'When you make your decisions think of me, and think of the person next to you in the same way as you think of yourself. Love like that.'

So we return to the place of the self. I believe God in Christ included our selves in his purposes of love, and asked us specifically to love our neighbours as we love ourselves. I fail to see how loving ourselves is the same as paying no attention to self and crossing out the 'I'. I believe that God is hinting that there is a perfect equilibrium to seek between himself, ourselves and our neighbours.

∾

It is interesting that during the years in which I tried to 'disappear', my body always mattered to me. I cared for it, valued it, laughed at it and enjoyed it. So in a strictly logical sense, part of the channel for God that I wanted to be, remained. There was still something of me left for God to occupy after I had ditched the essential 'I'.

Sitting on the 'I' was like sitting on a balloon. It wouldn't lie down. I became more self-conscious rather than less, until the balloon, under pressure from inside and out, burst.

My husband's proposal of marriage was like fresh air. His declaration of love for me fought against all the putting down of self that I had been standing for. There was no doubt that we loved each other. That he should love me enough to want to share his life with me was an affirmation and a direct appeal to my 'self', and was like air to the squashed balloon. I struggled to say 'yes' for a good half-hour. I did not understand why it took so long. I resisted his declaration of love at first and became unaware of what I was doing to him. I felt guilty, as though I shouldn't be loved. I spent many tortuous minutes trying to persuade him that I was not good enough and asking him if he was sure he really meant it. I could not believe that he loved me. Inside that struggle something else was stirring. I believe it was the truth. 'I' was still alive and responding to love. Eventually, I was able to perceive the reality underlying this 'performance'. My struggles and his ashen face gave way to a more positive scene. Eventually I got down off my high horse and agreed whole-heartedly to marry him. Thank heaven! That was thirty-nine years ago.

If that affirmation of love felt at first like a pressure to acknowledge the 'I' that I had been trying to hide, then there came a greater pressure later on. This time it was my body that suffered, the part of me I valued. I contracted chicken-pox on our honeymoon. It was a terrible blow to both of us, but to me it felt like a punishment. It was like an 'I told you so' from God for agreeing to marry such a famous man and so boosting my own ego in the process. The acquired sense of guilt for allowing myself such a luxury as being loved by somebody I adored had never really left me. What a mess! No wonder the balloon burst several months later, and I collapsed in an underground station drained of all my self-confidence.

That collapse was the beginning of a newer and more honest life, where love could begin to flow more freely, and where it became essential to learn to love myself and my neighbour, as God loved me. Looking back now I think what happened was the result of unwitting, but nevertheless real, self-indulgence. Concentrating on removing all traces of my ego was a way of indulging myself. In so doing, I was stifling the natural motivation that God had given me. All the 'I wants' that sprang up I had pressed down again and regarded as wrong. When I gave way to any desires, I had felt guilty, as though 'I want' was always wrong. Studying to be humble in that way had led to an arrogance that might have driven my fiancé away. Eventually it might have lost me the opportunity to love and be loved by a most loving person. His strong desire to love me, saved me. It set me on the road to a new life, and gave me the chance to get back in touch with a God who came to love and not to blame; who came to build up and not to pull down. It put me back in touch with reality. I had found the way back to the road towards self-respect.

PART II
RELATIONSHIP

Who is my neighbour?

5
Shame and Glory

Somewhere between shame and glory is a place of
proper pride where we can hold up our heads. It
is a place of dignity.

When our daughter was born, there was a good deal of media interest. One of my first thoughts following the joy of her arrival was that I must not let myself go. I set my hair and made up my face before the national press came to take the pictures they required. I did not want to let myself down. I thought that it was important to look good, to look dignified as opposed to dishevelled after my labours. We have pictures taken three days later and there is not a hair out of place.

Despite this self-consciousness and my wish to make a good impression, there was, I believe, a natural desire to redress a balance. My breakdown, five years previously, had hurt my pride. This was my chance to say to the world at large, 'You see, I am ordinary like you. I am a mother like you. I can function like a normal human being, like you. Please accept me back and forget my breakdown and all that is associated with those early days.' I still needed to reassure myself as well. I wanted to return to a place of dignity from a place of shame. What I came to realise later was that we never go back. We travel on to new places in the light of where we have already been. We have to own the shame experiences as much as the glorious ones. They are all part of the one journey.

During my experience of breakdown, shortly after David and I were married, I felt profound humiliation. Being admitted as a voluntary patient into a psychiatric clinic was the most humiliating experience I have ever had to face. I spent two days sobbing in my unsound-proof cubicle, feeling cut off, almost completely power-less, and all too aware of the anguished cries of the person next door. It felt like being in hell.

Someone came in to remove my belongings in case I did something silly like running away or damaging myself. That stirred something in me. I was furious. Shocked with ignominy, I asked the nurse to leave my things with me. I wondered what else they would take. I felt diminished and confused. I felt shamed, even though she was only doing her duty. She returned shortly afterwards and said I could keep them. A shred of self-respect returned, thanks to her willingness to take my request seriously. Being taken seriously at such times is important. It helped me to maintain my dwin-dling sense of identity and a degree of power and responsibility over my life.

After two days I emerged from my vale of tears, having become aware that I was not totally powerless. I had freedom of a kind. I was a voluntary patient and could leave at any time. I could ask questions about the treatments that I might have to undergo, and could set my terms. I did not have to submit to anything against my will. From somewhere in that valley of shame I discovered that I wanted to recover. Eventually I knew it would involve considerable effort and co-operation.

Choosing life when we are mentally sick is a difficult decision. On the one hand, life is the one thing that we want. On the other hand, the shame of being overtaken with such an illness can so envelop us that we are unable to hold up our heads or make any decisions for ourselves. Both energy and will run dry, and we hope for a magic and instant solution that will lift us back to be with everyone else who, we fancy, have no problems like ours, and who appear to be coping perfectly well.

As with a physical complaint, the need to attend to the problem and allow the healing to take place is the same. The difference is in the way we perceive the problems. In the 1950s when I broke down, psychiatrists were called 'trickcyclists' and 'shrinks'. We kept our distance by turning them into jokes. Mental sickness was something we hoped would not come near us. It was more of a mystery than breaking a leg, which was clearly visible. That mystery in itself was fuelled by ignorance, and our nervous joking did nothing to enlighten us. We simply did not want to know about it.

Nervous joking was one way of dismissing the fact that the mind as well as the body may need specialist attention. The other way was to deny categorically that there was anything wrong. Victorian expressions, like 'Snap out of it', and 'Pull yourself together', were offered as a solution by those who did not know any better. Sufferers were still left isolated in their struggle to cope with their lives. They were also made to feel that they were malingerers and public outcasts, people to be avoided.

Even now, when a home for mentally disturbed people is to be established, there is often a public outcry from the neighbourhood. There are fears that the value of property will fall. People fail to see how much they would have to gain by drawing closer to those who suffer in this way instead of keeping their distance.

All of us are flawed in some ways and dread rejection for reasons of weakness. So we strive to cover up that weakness by appearing strong, balanced and flawless. Distancing ourselves from the weak, whether they are ill or powerless for other reasons, only serves to feed our ignorance and prejudices. We will then be moving away from reality. Departing from truth like that has the effect of binding us instead of liberating us. We imprison ourselves in a world of our own making where everyone wears blinkers. We make fools of ourselves while making fools of others.

Wallowing in weakness is just as foolhardy as glorying in strength. It is only when we begin to acknowledge both sides of our humanity that we make room for moments of glory. Acknowledging moments of weakness or humiliation can be difficult, but so can acknowledging moments of glory. We sometimes find it hard to say 'thank you' graciously. We may find ourselves wanting to deny something good, or we become eager to retreat. But accepting moments of glory and praise in this life can be a foretaste of a greater glory while being part of our present reality.

I am slowly learning that humility is facing reality, and that I can accept praise without turning inner somersaults. Thirty-five years after my breakdown I found myself being given an honour publicly. When I was privately approached to see if I would receive an Honorary Fellowship of Liverpool Polytechnic (now the Liverpool John Moore's University), I blurted out awkwardly, 'Whatever for?' 'For your words, deeds, and for being yourself.' It had something to do with the way I handled fear.

During the intervening months before the ceremony, I worked to put aside my fears of many years depth – that I would panic, dry up, collapse, faint, lose control and become humiliated in some way. Comparing myself with others less favourably, as though we were in competition or in a market place, had to be cast aside as well.

I had to step into the spotlight as though it were the sunlight, and a sign of being wanted and affirmed. This affirmation came not only from people responsible in the Poly, but also, I believed, from God. I had to let myself go to that truth and stop fighting for more time and control. I decided to go for it. It was a time to be gracious.

Seated on the platform, I felt among friends. Looking down on the sea of faces I felt I was in the right place at the right time: I knew I must resist the ghosts from the past which nudged me to doubt that I should be there. (My mother has a biblical name for one of them, 'The accuser of the brethren'.) Today was a day for acceptance and not for accusations.

I had arrived at last at a place of dignity where I could hold my head up with proper pride. Although adrenaline played its part in my feeling of being fully alive, there was another ingredient. I had been given a taste of God's unconditional love, for I had not striven for this award. It was an unexpected gift, and I was slowly learning how to recognise and receive it graciously. Something about that day resonated deeply in my soul.

∾

Learning to move more easily from moments of shame to moments of glory will help us towards a more balanced and harmonious way of life. Facing our truth, whatever it is, we shall go on to live more creatively within ourselves and with others. It can be like managing the weights on some kitchen scales.

My mother still has her original spring balance kitchen scales. They are nearly sixty years old. They look old and worn, but they work perfectly, provided she places the kind of weights on them for which the scales were designed. Something from outside, placed on the metal plate above, responds to something inside. The result is shown on the large clock face. She has not been tempted to weigh a sack of potatoes on them, and they do not weigh letters. She has kept to the instructions and used her common sense. The integrity of the scales has not been damaged. They were well made. The spring mechanism has been oiled over the years. She has taken care of them. They work for her. It is as though the maker and the user understand one another.

This picture provides us with an image of how we can so easily upset each other's balance by using or abusing ourselves or one another. Problems would begin if a heavy load was placed on the scales. They would not last long. They were not designed to weigh everything in sight. In the same way we can make or break ourselves and one another by being heavy-handed in our dealings. Because we are not inanimate objects like the scales, we can see how important it is to live and work at understanding one another, while being truthful about ourselves.

Like the scales, we need to acknowledge that we have a good maker. We need a good authority and we need to know our limits. Our essential human dignity is bound up with the quality of loving and care that we have experienced from the day we were born. It depends on how we get on with other people. It depends on something we call relationship.

Relating to other people is vital if we want to grow through hurt and humiliation, and not leave ourselves isolated. Otherwise we can become bitter, lonely people, and we begin to make fools of ourselves, for the bitterness emerges in everyday behaviour. We can begin to diminish others out of our own unresolved hurt and shame. Nagging or destructive gossip, and putting others down behind their backs reflects what is going on inside us. We cease to be generous. We start withdrawing and erecting barricades around ourselves for protection. We shoot from the rooftops of our fortressed life. I know that I nag more at home when I am feeling less sure of myself, or belittled for some reason. Others put themselves down. They dismiss themselves as fools in their own eyes instead of facing up to the truth about their particular reality.

Such a threat to personal dignity feels like rejection and needs facing. Anticipating the worst is a way of defending ourselves against the pain we think will be intolerable. It will be the pain of humiliation. Not knowing is not being in possession of the facts. Finding out what facts there are helps to clear the mists of uncertainty, and prevents us from hurting each other unnecessarily and spoiling good relationships. In that sense the facts are kind. Knowing the worst may be painful, but less so than imagining the worst, and easier to deal with than wrestling with ghosts.

When we experience too much humiliation or too much affirmation that delicate balance is disturbed in us. We falter and lose our sense of proportion. On the one hand, too little attention to our needs leads us to be and to feel neglected. We can become fearful and defensive and our ability to live trustingly is affected. Like a sea-anemone, we shrink when we are touched. Our ability to love and be loved is eroded.

On the other hand too much attention can lead to self-centredness and arrogance. We can become spoilt and tempted to dethrone God and replace him with ourselves. There is a danger of becoming overbearing, boastful and dictatorial and inclined to bully other people, afraid of losing control. It does not take much to tip the scales.

All our relationships involve balancing. We have the power to make or break that delicate centre or spring balance that we call human dignity. This power is in the hands of both individuals and groups. Once again, like the scales, we deal in the receiving and the letting go of weights to find a balance. We are part of a creative activity with the power to disturb or restore, to break down or to build, to harm or to heal.

∾

Occasionally we experience a moment of wonder when everything holds together in creative harmony and we feel at one with ourselves, with one another and with the world outside. We have a glimpse of glory.

I once experienced one of these wonderful moments at a formal dinner. One of my neighbours was Sir Edward Boyle, at one time Secretary of State for Education. We had met years before at the Mayflower Family Centre in East London where David and I were living and working. In those days Edward Boyle was a well built, dependable and much loved friend to those working with young people in inner cities. He and I had not met since. On the evening of the dinner I had been informed that he was critically ill and weak with cancer, and was unlikely to last the evening. I was most apprehensive. I hoped he would not die that evening, and specially during one of our conversations, as I was unsure what would be required of me.

When he arrived I hardly recognised him. Gaunt and thin, he was a shadow of his former self. But there was a light in his eye as we sat down to eat. That light spoke to me of something lively. So I resolved to follow that light and put my fears behind me. I decided to look for something new that might have nothing to do with inner cities or cancer or youth work; something beyond the obvious labels.

At first he told me gently that he might have to leave before the end to get an early night. By the end of the evening I felt I had crossed the Rubicon. We had talked deeply and continuously about gardens and music, about family and faith: all things we both had in common. I forgot he was weak and dying. I felt as though we were two students back at college, free from our labels and released from our inhibitions. We found common ground by stepping on to it together and attending to each other. His interest in my world moved me, and brought me to life. My resolve to follow the light in his eye lifted me above myself, and we witnessed one of those moments of glory where each is enlarged by the other's presence and love, and both are set free to worship God.

He died shortly after that occasion. That experience changed my way of looking at people, especially when something about them frightens me. Edward Boyle helped me to see beyond the obvious to that which lightens every human being whatever their outward circumstances. We need to call that forth in each other if we want to go on to understand what glory means. We need times of closeness, and we need something or someone beyond ourselves to lift our horizons and give us hope when we feel fearful, overwhelmed or humiliated.

Moments of wonder like the one I described provide cameos of what glory means. 'You're wonderful!' we say. We little realise how many moments of wonder there are to witness each day in one another if we only have the will to look and the eyes to see.

We can recognise that happening between all sorts of people. I saw it once when I witnessed an exchange of greeting between a young person dressed as a punk and an elderly man who was a homeless traveller. After stopping to chat, they shook hands and waved goodbye and went on their way. I have seen it in the face of a much loved and severely disabled child who was being tenderly bathed by his father. On our television screens we see it in the face of a mother suckling her child while both their bodies are wasting away through famine. Sometimes sensitive media photographers capture these moments for us, but it is more real when we witness them first-hand, and can be partakers in moments of glory and not just observers.

Everyone is born with a light in the eye. It is the light of life, and the will to live. It is the torch of our essential dignity.

All of us are special enough to take responsibility for guarding one another's essential dignity, when it is threatened, as well as our own. If we do not take up this responsibility, then we fail each other. Each time any of us knowingly causes damage to the dignity of another person, the light of the world is diminished a little. By failing to act responsibly we contribute to the death of God's Image in the world. By preserving our relationship with one another, we make way for God's Spirit to move, and his glory to be revealed. By turning our backs on each other, whether between individuals or groups, we contribute towards the shutting down of life's resources.

There is no need to stand on our dignity, as though it would disappear. God's total attentiveness and unfailing love undergirding the world and its people is there. Even at times of degradation and humiliation and struggle, he is there in people, in his creation and beyond. All we are asked to do is to believe that, through thick and thin, and to go on looking for him.

When Christ was stripped of his clothing, his reputation and his belongings, he left us an example. Betrayed by a friend, physically bleeding and in mental agony, and banished outside the city wall, he cried out to God from that place of degradation and suffering, 'Why have you forsaken me?' Hardened soldiers, helmeted and powerful stood by observing. Women, grief-stricken and powerless, recognised that feeling of abandonment from their own experience. He had promised that it would not be the end. At that moment this promise remained a mystery, but it was something to hope for. Those women had to combine an honest outworking of their human feelings with a simple faith that there was to be glory somewhere, in the mystery of that suffering. And they were not alone.

I believe the way to life is somewhere between shame and glory. It is a place of dignity and light because Christ preserved that place for us and nothing can take it away. We can take courage and hope in dark times, knowing that we are not alone. We can bear one another's burdens. The glimpses of glory that we witness here are just glimpses of a greater glory that has yet to be revealed.

God's grace is not confined to the giving and receiving of awards, but lies waiting to be discovered in our ordinary everyday relationships, and in all creation. There is nothing more humbling and more enlivening, especially when it takes us by surprise. A simple kindness can change someone's life and outlook. A smile can make someone feel unexpectedly valued. A postcard sent at the right moment with a message of goodwill or thanks can make us feel that we matter just when we need it.

Relationship

When we put one another down by a remark, an action, or even by an attitude of superiority, then we contribute to a general reduction in human dignity in the wider community, and our will to live in harmony is dulled. We can gradually cease to care. Jokes in pubs or at dinner tables by white people about black people, derogatory remarks about people in their absence, refusing to believe that the disabled are capable of thinking and acting responsibly; these are attitudes that create division among ourselves instead of harmony. There are other, funnier things to make jokes about. We can so easily treat others as fools, but in doing so we make fools of ourselves. We have become unaware of our own arrogance and our fear of losing control.

We can start by accepting ourselves, and go on to respect one another. We can be open to surprises. Life is like a big conversation – it involves stories of both shame and glory. By welcoming the stories we welcome the storytellers and this is humbling and enlightening for all of us. A sense of neighbourhood, or mutual belonging, is deepened by this sharing. It is the beginning of a holy communion. Here we know we are not alone. Here we can have mutual respect in the presence of Christ and hold up our heads with dignity and proper pride.

6
Servility and Tyranny

Somewhere between servility and tyranny is a place
of mutual esteem where there is neither grovelling
nor bullying, but where effective service is given
and received by those who know their limitations.

Having moved away from the place of shame and
towards a place of greater self-respect and dignity, I
began to hold my head up, and to look more confidently
at people, at myself and at God. I began to believe that
I was not only cared for, but worth the caring. Once at
that place I became aware of two things. First I was
aware of having received something good, and then that
I might have something to offer. From despair I moved
to gratitude and on to service.

Without that transition from shame to feeling valued,
any attempts to serve others are likely to be patronising
and unhelpful. Without that movement to grow, there
is always a danger of becoming fossilised, like rocks, in
self-deprecation or self-righteousness. The place that I
seek lies somewhere between servility and tyranny:
between crawling and condescension.

∾

In my room I have a picture on the wall by the artist,
Peter Clare. It is one of his twelve Stations of the Cross
and is called 'Christ is stripped of his clothing'. This
picture of the suffering servant prompts me to question,
'Who is this Christ that we worship?' and 'Why do we

63

Jesus is Stripped of his Clothing by Peter Clare

worship someone who allowed himself to be treated like a criminal, and acquainted himself with such suffering and powerlessness?' 'Is Christianity masochistic?' 'Do I really have to go that way?' 'What is this life of service all about?' 'What kind of God is this?' I am bound to try to answer the questions.

In the centre of the picture is the diminutive figure of a bearded man, with one shoulder visible, who is having his scarlet robe removed by two soldiers: one on either side. The two tall soldiers are naked and tower over the central figure. Their heads are encased in huge metal helmets like upturned buckets. The central figure is wearing a crown of thorns.

Some of the answers to my questions lie in the figures of the soldiers. The rest remain in the constantly unfolding mystery of God, and of myself.

In the two soldiers depicted I find an absurdity that makes me laugh. It is the laughter of relief that comes when a picture slides into focus, when truth dawns. It is both liberating and illuminating.

They, like the central figure, are naked, vulnerable, open to hurt. The helmets speak to me of their role. They were only doing their job – paid to strip and crucify other men. The questions then become different ones. Do they know they are as vulnerable as their victim? Or, does wearing the helmet prevent them from seeing themselves as they are? Does being in role make them feel safer? Does it make them feel more powerful?

Answers emerge about the nature of God as seen in Christ. God became truly human, taking upon him our flesh. He became open to hurt, open to another's power, just as we are. He did not come to control, but to accompany and to serve. He gave us his life out of love for us, so that the penny of that truth would have a better chance of dropping. Peter Clare, in a recent exhibition of his paintings called 'The Journey', writes of seven years of his life when he was stripped of everything. 'Having come through that', he says of God's love, 'it is about the only thing of which I am certain.'

God came down to earth without losing his kingship, for he is both servant and king. No amount of serving could remove his crown. He risked misunderstanding of his role as an all-powerful God by wearing a crown of thorns, and also by putting a towel round his waist, and washing the feet of his disciples. Somehow he combined being completely human with being completely divine. This image of completeness could only be offered to us in human language for us to take or to leave. 'God with us' means exactly what it says, for a king can serve.

God knows about suffering. That we worship a God who knows about suffering and powerlessness will only be good news to those who suffer and feel overwhelmed. To others it will appear cranky and masochistic. To worship a God who depicts a man held hostage by his fellow men, will be good news to both men and women who feel imprisoned by the abuse of others. They will feel understood. To be presented with an image of God who was betrayed and deserted by his friends will be good news for lonely, abandoned people. They will feel less alone. To see a king not dripping with jewels and expensive clothes will be good news for poor people. They will not feel so distant. There will be a feeling of kinship and closeness. There will be less fear in the relationship between God and us, and more chance for love to enter in and be welcomed and exchanged.

But the penny of God's love will only begin to drop when we remember that Christ came not just to present images of God to us, but to show us the extent of God's love in human language and in service. He took the risk of intervening in our world and in our lives, because we were spoiling things through our lack of love. We had lost touch with our Creator and his kind of caring.

So we have our model. Effective service or caring involves coming alongside. It is personal and unpatronising. It is offered by those who leave us with freedom to choose. It is offered by those who are sufficiently aware of their own limitations and vulnerability, not from people on pedestals. It is offered by volunteers and professionals alike who know that they have limits and needs too, and are not too proud to receive help from others when necessary.

∾

One of the most significant places where mutual service occurs is in marriage. Here, certain vows are exchanged. Expectations are raised both in private and in public. Even then the 'mutual help and comfort' that we work for and expect in marriage only grows when there is underlying love and mutual respect in the relationship.

Marriage is a public demonstration of a private commitment. The service in public demonstrates that there is a corporate dimension to the couple's relationship, and that life does not begin and end with the private agreement.

Our marriage was more public than many because of David's involvement with the world of cricket. Captaining the England cricket team meant he was no longer a private person and neither was I. The national Press were present when we made our vows. This committed us even more to ensure that what we declared in public was also practiced in private.

Like most couples we have met times of turbulence in our relationship. These times have challenged us to look again at what we originally wanted and to take steps to move on to ground that preserved our freedom as individuals, yet which did not jettison the element of belonging to a partnership that we valued, and had freely entered years ago. As we have grown, our needs in those early days have developed into different needs. Although loving and mutual service still sat comfortably together, loving we discovered was more than talking and hugging. It also involved acknowledging and accepting weakness and vulnerability on both sides, and the giving and receiving of forgiveness and attention: of each esteeming the other. There was and is a cost to loving. We have to give something away in order to receive and grow. We have to give ourselves.

In 1957, like most brides then, I gave up my maiden name, and took on David's surname. I did that willingly. I gave up my job so that I was free to be 'a support' and 'a help' to my husband. Most people I knew thought this was acceptable, and right as well. He, on the other hand, continued with his work much as before, and the main difference for him was that he ceased to live alone. In that sense we both gave up our independence and resolved to live instead a life of interdependence.

But as time passed, it became clear that there was an imbalance in our relationship, and some changes were called for. I had him on a pedestal. He became the master and I the servant. I took over the duties of a housekeeper and, at the same time, became both a child and a mother to him. Somewhere in all that I lost myself. It was further complicated by that early breakdown following a bad attack of chicken-pox on our honeymoon.

In the early days of our marriage, as well as being a curate David was much in demand as a preacher. He was also recalled to play cricket for England. He was busy and often out in the parish and further afield. The servant in me was glad to be in the background, cooking, cleaning and maintaining our home. The child in me was disappointed that he was not at home to play more. The mother in me patronised and nagged him to take more time to relax, and wanted him to do well, particularly as I felt relatively useless due to my fears. Despite all that we were in love and enjoyed each other's company. But my breakdown forced us to look at aspects of ourselves that we might otherwise have preferred to avoid. We acknowledged our need of help. David accompanied me to the consultant psychiatrist, who skilfully engaged us both in work to do, even though I was technically the patient.

Through the services of that doctor, we were enabled to attend to our relationship in a way that enabled us both to grow up a little more as individuals and to grow together. David was exhorted to take holidays and regular days off, and to see the sense, when planning them, of taking into consideration our relationship as well as his work. I was encouraged to find ways of reclaiming myself.

Discovering my inner authority, and the ability to stay in the struggle of growing up, and doing this together with David, went hand in hand with feeling that I was worth something. I began to trust David when he told me he loved me, and not to entertain bitter thoughts that he married me because of some ulterior motive that I could not name. 'He's only saying that,' I used to think when he told me he loved me. I began to hold up my head again, and to face people, instead of shrinking from them. Our love flowed more freely and we felt supported. A new and more creative relationship began to strengthen and grow.

By this time we had moved to the Mayflower Family Centre in East London. David was warden, which made my role 'the warden's wife'. We were still in our twenties. Our flat was the first married home in a centre which accommodated thirty people. I did not like being 'just a housewife', and treated as a spare part whose only identity was wrapped up with being at home and mostly invisible to the people who lived there. Neither did I wish to be stereotyped as having a perpetual breakdown, when I was getting stronger every day. I felt I had more to give. My will to fight was returning; I had re-entered the struggle for life. It was a matter of pride that I accepted David's invitation to become a full member of staff. Like the chaplain's wife, I attended staff meetings, and shared the responsibilities of the Mayflower, without claiming a wage.

Living in a community like that, I wanted to play an active part and to make my contribution. I wanted to be part of the whole. There was work of all kinds to be done. Some of it was quite menial and unskilled. Answering the front door and the telephone, tending the garden, helping in the hostel kitchen, staffing the youth club, cleaning out drains, playing the piano in chapel, sweeping up, helping with group outings and church holidays, visiting, poster making, entertaining, leading Bible studies and taking confirmation classes; these were some of the duties. I also conducted a men's choir.

Belonging to the staff group for twelve years, and being given the opportunity to contribute to that community from a position of human weakness, gave me more than a dozen training courses and many waged jobs would have done. (I did not need the extra money.) I was given the dignity of joining, structurally, a community that I already belonged to. I did not have to fight for a place. The great fear of someone who has experienced a breakdown is that they will be broken off, or thrown on the scrap-heap like rubbish. To be accepted, and included like that, was one of the greatest healing forces I have known.

I learned to bring my own skills, and to believe they were acceptable. This became easier as I learnt that the others were human too and did not hide their vulnerability from the rest. This was largely due to George Burton, the Scot from Glasgow that I mentioned earlier, who through his unshakable faith and transparent humanity forced us to be honest with ourselves and to be aware of the forgiveness and love of God when we found we were becoming angry, irritable, tired, hurt or frightened. We learned to face human reality together, and I am certain this made us humbler people. No one could stay on their high horse for long; it became hilarious all too soon, and we laughed a lot. We also cried.

Through serving the local people together, we received from them. As we worked and prayed, we found ourselves serving one another, sustaining, maintaining, holding, listening. When one suffered, we all suffered. When one rejoiced, we all rejoiced. When one was ready to pack his bags and leave, the rest would feel it and hold the ropes. For we all lived under the same roof – and our welfare lay in each other's welfare. We shared a common vision. We knew what we wanted. Our purpose in being there was to enable a local church to be established.

Arriving at Canning Town with my middle-class attitudes of superiority, I soon learnt some tough and important lessons about prejudice, which in the end is about forming judgements out of ignorance. George, our Scottish colleague, soon ensured that we were educated, till we were able to see that a person's language is a natural expression of where he or she springs from, and is neither right nor wrong. I vividly recall a toddler in one of our Mums' groups who was looking for her teddy bear. 'Cor, mum,' she said, 'where's my bleedin' bear?' From my relatively sheltered upbringing I was shocked to hear such a small child speak like that, yet soon came to accept that it was the only language she had known and was therefore as natural as my own, and probably more fitting. It was none of my business as a serving person in that community to correct her, or to make her speak like me. That would have been to introduce an element of control and interference that would have been quite inappropriate and unquestionably arrogant.

We Christians are exhorted to have a sober estimate of ourselves, esteeming others more highly, and yet also to love ourselves; to look up to others, and not to look down on them, as though they were lesser mortals. Christianity is paradoxically both a building-up and a coming-down religion. Christ's own example included the building up of those who were broken, like the bereaved, the sick and the vulnerable. It included the breaking down of those who considered themselves to be wise in their own eyes, who were hypocrites, and those who wielded power to abuse the poor, the weak and the powerless, and to oppress them. In the end tyranny defeats itself.

Yet serving does not necessarily mean I must be a doormat. I was speaking recently with a woman who was an academic when she married her clergy husband. She was telling me that some time after her husband's death, she realised that she had colluded with the notion that her role was to do entirely with what other people wanted, including her husband. She had rarely stepped outside her role. Then, during her time of grieving, she came to a point where she realised that there was a 'self' inside waiting to be born. That realisation was the beginning of a great release. 'I felt I needed my own space,' she said. Having known her before her bereavement, I could see that she had given birth to the self she spoke of. As a person she was like someone freed and unchained from others' expectations. She was not driven to serve by a fear of disapproval any more. She was free to choose, and her gifts were released. Her new inner stillness made her a much easier person to relate to. She was more alive, more responsive. Had her collusion been a form of humility? Was her wish to give birth to the self an arrogant wish? I do not believe so.

Christ called us friends not slaves. Slavery was, and is, enforced and is a total submission to power and authority. In the days of slavery power resided in the hands of a master and all the slave was expected to do was to obey. He had no freedom. His will did not count. Disobedience would often mean death, and an end to the relationship.

Friendship is different from slavery. There is a greater flexibility between the two people. Power is exchangeable. Ideally, powerlessness and vulnerability are also shared. There is mutual respect, and mutual recognition of need. The preservation of the relationship is important. The freedom of each person to choose, to opt in and to opt out, is nurtured, and life and energy can both ebb and flow like the tides. More life is generated and energy is created outside itself.

Sometimes it is difficult to be on the receiving end of another's kindness, or of some privilege. What have I done to deserve this? we ask, as though it were some reward. Being served like that makes us feel in debt. We lose something, and often fly to replace that loss by giving something in return to cancel the debt. It has taken me years to accept that to say 'Thank you' is enough. It does not need to be followed immediately by a *quid pro quo*, or by a sense of guilt. Life is not meant to be a series of business transactions where we do deals with one another. We do not have to pay back or give back what we have been given. We can receive and be thankful. We can give, expecting nothing in return. If living is to be loving, then each time a friend rings up with some encouragement, or someone gives me a jar of homemade marmalade for instance, all I need to do is to say 'Thank you'. The result of such simple acts of kindness adds to my store of being valued and loved, and it is that which makes me want to show my love to others out of love, and not out of duty. Kindness, mutual service and loving begins to flow freely and unconditionally.

∾

I would like to rehabilitate the word 'service'. There is a concept of service that can and does inspire us to offer and receive friendship without fear of betrayal; neighbourliness without fear of abandonment, and service without the loss of dignity. One of the keys to this place is to be found in the notion of vocation, or a special calling.

A Christian vocation means that we become aware that God is calling us individually to a particular piece of service that is likely to require a degree of self-sacrifice. It is not only about ordination to the ministry, the religious life, or overseas missionary work. In the secular world, professions like teaching and nursing used to be referred to as vocations. There is motivation over and above the usual wish to work. It is always to do with serving other people, usually involving lower than average pay, and it needs to be tested.

Vocation underlines the initial desire to serve. Those who respond and test their calling usually expect to stay with that calling for life through good times and bad and whatever conditions prevail. Those with a sense of vocation carry a certainty of their call and are also possessed by a peculiar drive to pursue their calling. The calling is compelling and, for those of us who are religious, we are aware of the one who called us. Vocation ensures the continuing of service but not always the pay.

We all experience service every day of our lives. The milkman and the postman bring us milk and mail without fail through wind and weather. Power and water are supplied to our homes and institutions to bring light and heat. Our bins are cleared of rubbish each week and our roads are swept, often while we sleep. This basic provision for our needs goes a long way to ensure that as communities and as a society we are civilised and ordered to some degree.

When we are sick, there are doctors, dentists and nurses, hospital and hospice staff to care for us. When we want our babies baptised, or we want to be married or need to be buried, the church is there to offer those services in every parish in the land. When our children, or we ourselves, want to learn, the teaching profession is there in our schools and colleges, trained and ready to help.

Faithful reliable service can make all the difference between order and disorder. Fluctuating, short-term, or reluctant service can destabilise us, so that we are forced back into our corners of self-sufficiency and self-reliance, instead of being able to rely on each other in a fluid giving and receiving of mutual service.

I prefer travelling in my car because it is more reliable than public transport. But car travel means that instead of travelling together we travel alone. We take the strain that could be eased by another's willing and gifted service. We choose to bear our own burdens, whether it is old age, the need for housing, or sickness. We have created an alternative, 'do-it-alone' society where we hide our needs, and hope that no one else will notice until they are forced to.

This self-sufficiency is not all destructive, but too much of it can lead to isolation and loneliness. It is no wonder that many resort to another world where they feel more valued and less alone. The world of crime offers one alternative. So does the world of drugs and sexual licence. Those worlds may offer an exciting shop window to some, but in reality a person soon finds out that he or she is not valued in those worlds as a human being made in God's image. Nor are they made to bring life and energy to others through service freely given and accepted.

In the world of work we are laying each other off, slimming down our work forces and closing opportunities to make a contribution to the whole. Through this approach we have literally let each other down from a place of dignity and mutual self-esteem. We deny offering a signal of another's worth by paying a fair wage. Instead some have to queue to receive 'benefit', 'credit' or dole, like beggars. On top of that experience, we expect our neighbours to hold up their heads with some dignity, despite the charge if they are unemployed of being scroungers or workshy. This is a kind of societal abuse, and we should not be surprised at large-scale signs of instability. It is of our own making.

Living in East London during the 'fifties and 'sixties, and later in Liverpool since the 'seventies, I have become acutely aware of the ignominy that many people experience when the choice to work is removed. Removing opportunities on a large scale to contribute to the community by working dehumanises us all in the long run.

Professional work brings in a wage, and money is necessary as it helps us to buy things that we need and value. Money is also society's principal way of showing what it values. It is a language and a way of saying 'thank you' and 'well done'. It is a way of saying on behalf of all of us, that we need and want each other's service for our mutual welfare and survival. Money speaks. Like it or not, it is the language of value in our culture. When it is removed or replaced with less, the message is clear. It says either, 'I don't need you any more,' or, 'What you are doing is not needed as much as it used to be.' Built into these messages is rejection and abandonment. When we are rejected or abandoned something rises up in us. We feel indignant and begin to complain. We must not be surprised when that happens. What was a civilised conversation between people changes into conflict; inevitably there is protest.

If the conversation between those who authorise the dole and those who receive it, turns into conflict, then a dangerous division is set up. Two sets of values and two sets of people begin to emerge and we have a split society, not at ease with itself.

So much depends on who or what we worship. If we worship money our values will be dictated by that; we will live for money. If we worship a God who loves people, or we simply believe in people, then we shall see things in a different light. Our values will not depend on money, for our treasure will lie elsewhere. Our motivation will be different. We will see the value of serving one another, either in professional or voluntary work, and will feel at peace in our heart of hearts because we know it is right and healthy.

It is in this context that voluntary work makes sense. Here less money exchanges hands. People who want to work without claiming a wage usually have enough money to live on. Yet something motivates them to want to contribute their time, their expertise and also their money to help others.

Although I worked as a teacher for a short time, most of my life I have been involved in voluntary work. My motivations have been mixed. There have been times when I have taken on tasks because I have been too weak to resist requests rather than because I wanted to do them. At other times I have become involved out of fear that I might be regarded as lazy if I did not have something like that to show for my privileged life. But most of all there has been a strong and recurring drive to give, out of sheer gratitude, something in return for all the gifts I have received.

Recalling the struggles that my mother endured during the war has made me aware today of the many young single parents with poor health who have to manage a young family alone without partner, friends, extended family or adequate money. Often, like my mother in those days, they must visit their children in hospital without telephone or transport, and with no nearby extended family or friends to support them. This awareness is strong and informs my attitudes and questionings. I am naturally interested in who is there for them. How do they cope with dignity? Who helps them without making them feel that they are a burden? Who helps them to rediscover their strengths and self-confidence to cope again? Who is there when life threatens to overwhelm them?

These were the questions that led me to agree to be associated with the Family Service Unit in Liverpool. I believe I was approached for several reasons. I was the new bishop's wife and I know new bishops' wives are targeted for such tasks. Tempted as I was to be the person to befriend the families myself, rather as I befriended my own mother as a small child, I realised that this was unrealistic if not arrogant. There were others who had taken the time and trouble to train for the task. Who was I to think I could do it better, or even as well? There were professional social-work staff and therapists whose training equipped them to ensure a proper detachment between client and worker in emotionally draining circumstances. My job therefore became clear. It was to support the professional people in any way I could. This would mean being willing to attend committee meetings, to raise funds, and to use my public position to make contacts with influential people and to keep them informed.

Working in a voluntary organisation in this way has been most rewarding. It has also tested my motivation to its limits. Did I really want to serve the families, or did I want to be able to boast about my good works? Did I really want to raise funds for the organisation, or did I want to show off and demonstrate what a hard-working bishop's wife I was? These questions arose and I had to answer them truthfully. At first, as I have said, my motives were mixed. After a while the glamour of the new involvement wore off and the work became increasingly demanding. Discussing issues like conditions of service or a budget in a committee, was not what I had originally hoped to do. It appeared to be more about the staff than the families. Yet I quickly came to realise that if the staff are not properly supported and paid, then the clients suffer. It is the responsibility of both staff and committee to communicate sufficiently out of mutual respect. This way encouragement can be released and a good service can be delivered.

Seeing people in need evokes an emotional response in most of us. I often want to drop what I am doing and run to help, thinking that I know what is needed. Others turn to blame. Most of us want to do something to change the pain and suffering that we see. Our common humanity cries out in empathy and sympathy.

But some ways of helping can reduce a person's dignity; there are other ways that retain it. Fools rush in where angels fear to tread, and rushing can overwhelm a person, leaving him or her no room to think for themselves. There needs to be a realistic assessment of what the needs are, including careful listening to the person or people concerned. It is then possible to give a consistent, accountable service that is acceptable to the person on the receiving end. Family Service Units all over the country approach their work with this attitude. Social workers, medical staff and others in the caring professions can make all the difference to a person's self-esteem by the way they do their service.

Somewhere between servility and tyranny is a place of mutual esteem where there is neither grovelling nor bullying, but where effective service is given and received by those who know their limitations, and who respect each others' gifts.

7
Isolation and Involvement

*Somewhere between isolation and involvement is
a place of healthy detachment. Here we can
acknowledge our interdependence without either
crowding or abandoning one another.*

Just after World War II broke out, my mother and
brother and I were evacuated from London to Milton
Keynes. We were isolated from the big city with its
hustle and bustle of people and traffic, and from the
threat of bombs. We were also separated from my father
and his work in the parish. We had no telephone, no
transport and the nearest shops were in Newport Pag-
nell, five miles away.

At that time Milton Keynes was only a village and
there we began to live in a more intimate community.
The air was clearer, and my brother and I could play
with friends in the countryside. It was quieter and
cleaner, and my mother's asthma began to subside. We
had a garden, and we learned how to grow vegetables.
There were fewer people immediately around us than
in the city.

For three years we enjoyed being an ordinary family,
albeit a one-parent one, as my father had to remain in
London to care for the parish. Later he volunteered to
serve in the Army abroad, and we saw him even less.
We had to learn to manage without him and to make
new friends. We could involve ourselves as much or as
little as we liked in the village, unlike in the vicarage,

where the parishioners used our home as their own on occasions, and as children we were caught up in the wider community of a parish. My father was in his element, but for my mother, keeping such an open home sometimes had felt overwhelming. She had been struggling with asthma in the London smogs and felt she was losing control of her breath as well as her home. We had felt the pain of her experience.

So evacuation became a happy isolation for us children and a time of relative freedom for my mother. But we were cut off in other ways, and later we moved to a place where there was more choice of schools and where we could learn to mix more widely.

During those three years at Milton Keynes, at the age of seven I was isolated further when admitted to hospital to have my tonsils removed. There were complications and I became ill with jaundice and a collapsed lung. I was moved to a room by myself where I was weak and miserable, and later to an emergency hospital. I was away from my family for ten weeks, and I missed them and the presence of other children.

This enforced isolation was painful for me. Isolation can, though, sometimes be a relief. It can be something we long for as well as something we dread. It can be a relief, for example, when we have become over-involved with other people. On the other hand, it can hurt when we are cut off against our will through illness, desertion and punishment. We feel the pain of isolation more keenly after knowing closeness and intimacy in our relationships.

Too much isolation is dangerous, for we can become self-absorbed, and instead of visits from people being welcome, these can begin to feel like interruptions. On the other hand, too little solitude can arouse a fear of being alone and bring us to a state where we feel content only when we have company, and are miserable when left to ourselves. It is a balance between isolation and involvement that we seek; not too much and not too little. It will depend on our experience how much or how little of each we shall need from day to day. When we arrive at that balance, we shall experience a healthy detachment. This detachment will acknowledge an essential interdependence without either crowding or abandoning one another as we grow. As individuals we will be comfortable with either.

Part of the experience of isolation can be loneliness. Although a belief in God means that we are never alone, we can still feel lonely. Few of us like to admit that, yet to admit it to ourselves is the first step to combating it. This frees us to do battle with loneliness, if we wish. Accepting that feeling, we can then look at the reality and decide what we want to do.

For the last twenty years I have lived in a large house which is set in two-and-a-half acres of ground. It is my home and I love it. My neighbours are not within shouting distance. Sometimes I am alone in the house and, though not frightened, I would prefer to have nearer neighbours. One day during a particularly busy spell, I became dizzy. Unable to keep my balance I decided to lie on the floor. I was there for over an hour, and despite my efforts, I could not ease myself to a telephone or to the panic button to ask for help. It was a time of extreme loneliness because I felt helpless to do anything for myself. It is surprising what inspiration even a ceiling brings when there is little else to look at. Eventually I decided to relax my body and accept the situation. By the time my husband returned home, I was physically still unable to move, but less panicky and therefore able to distinguish fact from fantasy. He helped me onto the bed and called the doctor. Eventually the dizziness subsided. All I needed was a couple of days' rest.

Many people have to cope alone day after day, without a partner, friend or doctor to come to their aid. No one knows what they are facing. Some even die alone. That is a tragedy, and is something we rightly fear. We can be isolated in our own homes, in communities and even in countries. We need a way of communicating our need to others, and then we will have to exercise humility to accept help when it comes.

The thought of dying alone is frightening for most of us. But we cannot have it both ways. If we have been accustomed to being independent, and not beholden to anyone, then it will be difficult to surrender that independence. It will feel like an offence to our dignity to begin to submit to the ministrations of others. It will disclose some of our weakness, which is what independence hides so successfully.

But dying alone is not the ultimate dread. In the end we fear that we will be rejected – rejected by God. That would be the supreme isolation. 'My God, my God why have you forsaken me?' Yet this cry from the founder of our faith is a clue to why we are never in fact alone. Christ has been to the darkest pit of all. His life-giving spirit has returned to reassure us of his presence during times of deep loneliness. His spirit brings acceptance and understanding of our fears which helps us to face them. His life on earth also gave us clues as to how we could prevent such loneliness and isolation happening.

One of those clues is through involvement with others, particularly the forgotten, the disregarded and the physically and mentally weak. By isolating them we isolate ourselves. Our welfare lies in their welfare, for there, but for the grace of God, do we go. But initially we are afraid of involvement with such people, unless we have a vocation to serve them in one of the professions or in a voluntary capacity. We are afraid that if we keep company with those on the margins we will become marginalised ourselves: that if we live near mentally handicapped people this may affect our own sanity: that if we fraternise with poor people then somehow our own well-being and even our bank-balance will be affected. But this must be confronted for our own good for, in the end, this kind of involvement is a legitimate self-interest.

Giving in to our fears and fantasies puts us out of reach of one another. Like me in our house, we are out of shouting distance. Weakness, illness and unkindness are part of the human condition. Christ's way was to be human and to get as close as he could to the people who suffered, and to listen to them. Nowadays the issues include drug and alcohol abuse, HIV and AIDS, poverty and crime. Those who work closely with the sufferers of AIDS tell us how much they learn about kindness and self-sacrifice from their patients. Social workers tell us of the courage of some of their clients in the face of many odds. Those who come alongside the poor discover what real caring can be like, as the poor are often far more generous with the little they have than those of us with more. Keeping our distance can make us arrogant and prejudiced; we may tell others who suffer how they should behave without truly knowing what we are talking about.

Keeping our distance is one way of dealing with our fears, but it does not work. On the other hand, becoming more involved dispels ignorance and fear, and brings a new freedom. For example, I was once invited to spend an evening with the l'Arche Community in Liverpool. l'Arche provides a permanent home for severely mentally handicapped adults. I was quite anxious about going. I imagined that my awkwardness might disturb the people I was to meet, and their behaviour might be beyond my control. I was afraid of being embarrassed or of showing myself up. I was afraid of my own ignorance.

In the event I need not have worried. Their graciousness dispelled my fears. There was a dignity in their bearing that shone through. They were simply themselves. Their childlike transparency was refreshing. It encouraged me to be open too and to come down off my pedestal of so-called normality and join them round the meal table without my airs and graces. Over the meal each person was given an opportunity to say something. Everyone was noticed. Because l'Arche had made room for them, they made room for others like me. A two-way bridge had been created instead of a wall, and they had begun the building of it. I came away humbled and enlightened and with a different view of mentally handicapped people. I was fearful no more.

However, another way of letting our fears get the upper hand is by becoming over-involved. Often this happens because we cannot say 'no'. We find we cannot say 'no' to others and 'yes' to ourselves for fear of being selfish. So in saying 'yes' to everyone else, we are saying 'no' to ourselves and call it unselfishness. We then lose sight of our need for a more rhythmical and balanced life. Over-committed at work and with little energy for a private life, we secretly long for time to ourselves and become jealous of others who manage it. We lose touch with our family and friends, and we lose touch with ourselves. It becomes hard to slow down and take stock. It is like losing the use of brakes. We run the risk of a crash, or a breakdown, or we 'burn out'.

Saying 'no' is not always as negative as it sounds. I have had to learn to say 'no' to others more often, and to make room for my own interests. This has acted as a counter-balance to an over-busy life where time for maintaining personal relationships can be squeezed out by a disordered set of priorities. Creating space is like walking on the Yorkshire hills after shopping in a crowded centrally heated store. It brings life like fresh air. I have had to learn that a bursting diary speaks, but it does not necessarily tell how hardworking I am. It may be saying that I am escaping from something, or that I am afraid to slow down. It may be indicating that my brakes have failed and that I need help. We need to apply our brakes as well as the accelerator to have a good and safe journey.

Sitting still does not always mean being lazy. Once I can remember stuffing behind a cushion a woman's magazine that I was reading, when I heard the front door bell ring. The thought in those days of being caught relaxing made me feel guilty. From somewhere I had gleaned the idea that I ought to be working, and be seen to be working, every waking hour. Since then, I have been enabled to see the folly of such behaviour. What matters is whether I am stewarding my life properly, not what it looks like to others.

To turn down invitations to speak, for instance, does not mean I am ungracious. But there are temptations. As well as being a challenge, being asked to speak can be flattering and can make me feel wanted and valued. This can sweep me off my feet and cause me to accept when I know there is not the time for preparation. I will then be acting under undue pressure. Or I can panic and begin to believe that if I say 'no' this time they will never ask me again. This kind of panicking shows that I would be afraid that one of the sources of my self-esteem would dry up. To yield to this kind of temptation means that I remain on the helter-skelter and let it take me, hoping that it will do the stopping for me. It is all

87

right to have a ride on the helter-skelter sometimes, but to ride on it every day is not to take life seriously. It means we do not value this precious gift, but are in danger of abusing it. Then it is less likely that we will understand the true meaning of love which involves commitment, effort and discipline. Life is fun, which is not the same as treating it as a perpetual playground.

It is all very well learning to say 'no' to people and their demands, but for some, that can be all too easy. For them, saying 'yes' is much more of a challenge. For example, Carlos Valles* tells of a nun he knew who was afraid of cars. This fear became something of a phobia. She found it difficult to cross a street even at a green light, and crossing a main road without traffic lights was a major challenge. There was something behind this fear of cars. It turned out to be a fear of people, moving units on the road of life. She feared company, feared dialogue, feared encounters of any kind, feared living in a group. It was difficult for her to say 'yes', and this was disabling for her. Valles goes on to say, 'To be rejected is the ultimate condemnation. No wonder that in order to avoid such a gloomy possibility, we may at times inhibit ourselves, draw back and choose solitude. But the price of solitude is greater than the pain of rejection.'

Saying 'yes' and 'no' in the right places can reduce the problem of over-involvement and, at the same time, can prevent us from becoming cut off from our fellow human beings. It can also be a sign that we are learning to love ourselves more effectively. Learning to love ourselves prevents us from relying on others all the time for a sense of worth. It makes room for a healthier and more fulfilling way of life. Then we can affirm our-

*In *Let Go of Fear*, Triumph 1991.

selves more and lower our expectations of others to a more realistic level. But that depends on how we see God and whether we relate that image to people and view them with his eyes. We are made in his image.

When teaching myself to venture out alone again, I went to catch a train. I had tried the previous week and failed, returning home exhausted and punctured with a sense of failure. The night before my second attempt, we had a visitor, Gerard W. Hughes, the author of *God of Surprises*. His writings had played an important part in my development. They had reintroduced me to the love and tenderness of God at the right time. That evening I thanked him and told him of my failure the previous week to board the train. He said, 'The facts are kind.' He asked me if I had thought of viewing the trainload of people as though they had been made in the image of God; accepting, loving, healing, friendly. I confessed I had not. I was inspired to try once more.

The following day I stood on the platform, determined to believe that the people on the train were made in the image of a kind and friendly God. Trembling and perspiring, I knew he had pointed to some truth. Leaving my place of long isolation, I stepped on to the train. As soon as my second foot left the platform, my fear evaporated. The train moved out of the station and I felt among friends. I sat down and the person opposite gave me a friendly smile which I returned. At last I had begun to trust the better side of people instead of treating them as enemies. Instead of turning away from people out of fear of rejection, I had begun to involve myself again as a vulnerable human being among others, believing the best. Physically I felt taller, and the blood flowed more easily and warmly in my veins. The problem has not returned.

Everyone has the capacity to be kind and helpful.

Instead of living solitary lives in a climate of distrust and fear, we can treat people as friends and help to create a community of individuals who know and respect each other's vulnerability, and who are there to help in time of need.

Accepting that vulnerable part of being human means taking care that we look at real hurts and not imagined ones. Doing this involves a detachment which gives us a clearer view. We need to stand back a little and respect our varying needs and make room for each other to be ourselves. Standing too close can stifle and prevent healing taking place. We need to arrive at a place of detachment.

Like the plants and animals we need air, both physical and emotional air. We need time to breathe and space in which to grow. When others cannot give it to us we must seek it for ourselves. We also need closeness. Sitting alone at home with the television or radio for company is all right for a while, but they can be sterile companions in the long term. We need a balance of isolation from and involvement with other people.

At home we have a sofa opposite the television set. At the end of the day David and I sit down and relax together on it. When we have something particular to sort out there are at least four options of ways of relating to one another. First, we can slump down side by side and watch what comes next, avoiding the issue. Secondly, we can start to talk about our day while watching the screen at the same time, half-listening. Thirdly, we can sink all our problems and joys in one big embrace and forget the television altogether. This may solve one problem but leave the other untouched. Or, when there are particular issues to sort out, we can, perhaps after watching the news, agree to sit opposite one another and talk face to face, with a little more distance between us. When we take the last option, and look at each other in the eyes, we obtain a more balanced view of the subject in hand and reach a more satisfactory conclusion. The choice is ours each time.

Personal detachment can also be achieved in extreme circumstances, by becoming our own observers. Brian Keenan tells of his battle with insanity while in captivity as a hostage in Beirut. In this powerful account of struggling to maintain a lively balance during enforced isolation, he says,

> I decided to become my own self-observer ... I allowed myself to be and say and think and feel all the things that were in me, but at the same time could stand outside observing and attempting to understand. I would let myself go and watch myself, full of laughter, become the thing that my mind was forcing me to be.*

Detachment is a tool, and helps to restore or keep a sense of balance to prevent us from the dangers of dwelling in the extremes of destructive isolation or suffocating involvement. But we must not forget to laugh at what we see. It can be very funny, and laughter brings us down to earth again.

An Evil Cradling, Hutchinson, 1992.

PART III
LIVING

*How can we love
one another?*

8
Certainty and Doubt

*Somewhere between certainty and doubt there is a
place of commitment with exploration. Here we
can enjoy unravelling mysteries together.*

We tend to regard doubt as something to avoid. Certainty sounds more positive, yet we can glory too much in either, to our cost. A healthy acquaintance with both can lead to commitment which incorporates an element of adventure and exploration.

There was a time when I was afraid of flying. Fear of the unknown prevented me from trying, and trusting myself to be airborne in a huge heap of metal did not seem feasible. I had flown once before, and it was an unpleasant and bumpy ride and associated with a difficult time in my life. After that I was content to do my travelling abroad by sea and to explore no further.

Then came an opportunity to go to America. This seemed too good to turn down as we were invited as a family. But that first flight had set up fears again that I did not think I could handle. It set up doubts.

Eventually with the encouragement of my family and my underlying wish to travel with them, I agreed to go. With my husband and daughter on either side, we held hands, and I made my frozen legs walk on to the plane. The fear was converted into the original excitement as the idea of flying turned into reality and the wheels of that great aircraft left the ground. We drank champagne which was the gift of a friend for this occasion.

The world opened up to me. Looking down on the earth below, my earlier struggle suddenly seemed distant and unimportant. Houses looked like pieces from a Monopoly board, and rivers like ribbons. But that struggle with fear was vital to my growth. Without it I would still be on the ground, dreaming of adventure but never committed to it. Without taking the opportunity to discover how much I wanted to fly I would have been left with all doubt and no certainty over whether I could. Now I know I can. I love it. But I still do not fully understand how the aeroplane stays in the air; I just know that it does. Knowing that I was supported and loved became my launch pad. Those certainties had outweighed the doubts at last. All I had to do was to supply the will and the action, and to put down my pride, or the fear of making a fool of myself.

All doubts and no certainty undermines confidence. Too much self-doubt prevents us from trusting ourselves to others with any degree of commitment. We become shy and retiring and apt to apologise for who we are and what we do. We become afraid and reluctant to be ourselves.

On the other hand too much self-assurance can mean that we find it difficult to acknowledge weakness, to ask for or to accept a helping hand, or to climb down after an argument. There we believe we are self-sufficient, in the right, and have nothing to learn. We do not like to bother others with our needs. We stand on our dignity. Refusing to apologise, for instance, can prolong a rift between people, sometimes for years.

We need a balance between doubt and certainty to find a place of positive growth and energy. In that place of energy we are more ready to commit ourselves to one another in lively, loving relationships and in a life of exploration and adventure.

∾

Our world is full of treasure that lies waiting to be unearthed. That world is God's gift to us and we can make it work. There is always more to explore. But too often we become tempted to draw back from the challenge to confront the mystery of life. So we play safe and avoid the risk of adventure. We lose out on the opportunity to grow in confidence and knowledge. We fear complexity. We fear not being able to cope. We fear losing control.

Complexity can complicate our clear view, and confusion threatens our certainties. But we would be foolish to suggest that real life includes no clouds. Clouds can be part of a beautiful landscape. We need to look complex issues full in the face, staying with confusion while remembering that it is a stage in the journey. Muddle can indicate a loss of control, a loss of authority and of leadership. The world does not understand a confused Christian. Neither does it trust an over-confident one. Even less does it accept a doubting bishop. These appear to be contradictions in terms. 'Give us a lead,' is the cry, a pleading for authoritative words of conviction that make things clearer.

But religious people who are not honest about being confused give a false impression of the truth. Bishops who have no doubts have stopped asking questions. This pleading for certainty is a sign of inner confusion and the loss of a good authority within. When I am at my most insistent for someone else to be clear, it means that I am confused myself.

When someone is set up as an authority on religion or morality, there can be a temptation to leave issues of right and wrong to them. We hand over our responsibility for sorting out our muddles and confusions to others. This abdication means that we think we can knock our authority figures down again when we do not like what they say, like a child playing with a pile of bricks. It becomes a game.

For some, any suggestion that doubt may be part of a living faith, should be howled out of court. Doubt complicates things, they say. Religion, we are told, is a matter of simple faith, and anyone who dares to question old truths and make things complicated is coming close to heresy. Bishop David Jenkins, former bishop of Durham, a firm believer in God and Christ, is an example. He has raised questions about issues like the Virgin Birth and the Resurrection which have been exploited out of context by the Press. He has made us think. The doubts he has introduced are not new to the professional, yet the cherished convictions of some religious people have been shaken.

Suddenly we Christians have to do our thinking in public, and those unused to reasoning their faith out loud find themselves in a place of confusion and of some embarrassment. It is painful for them. This can set up a spiritual agoraphobia where the market place feels frightening, so we retreat into our corners and hang on for dear life to what we know, for fear of losing what little we have. Fear is love gone rigid.

This can happen to any of us at any time. We need to respect each other's position as we will be in different places on the journey, and we will have arrived there by different routes. So it is important on all sides, to do some listening before plunging in with our arguments. The special ingredient of respecting love can create a genuine dialogue out of a painful encounter. That way the essential dignity of each can be preserved and the truth discovered.

When I was in my twenties and a devout Christian, I owned a small Bible with a black leather cover. I read it regularly, carried it with me, and marked it in places. One day I found myself in an argument over which was the original version. Although I had learned in school about the existence of earlier versions, the truth that my Bible was not the original had not dawned on me. I had come to believe that the Authorised Version was the earliest and most reliable. I almost worshipped my own copy. When this was challenged by a close friend, I found myself resisting the idea with passion. The Revised Standard Version was in circulation, and I could not bring myself to accept it. I struggled and argued with my friend until at last, like the sunrise, the truth dawned.

I began to accept that of course there were other versions before the Authorised one. History proves that beyond doubt. New scholarship means new insight. The original was not set in tablets of stone. My Bible had grown out of the scholarship of years, and would be succeeded by others. I was ashamed of my ignorance.

After a fierce argument, I realised I was fighting a losing battle, and was showing how much I had been accepting without question. I broke down in sobs of bereavement and then of relief. I felt I was losing something that I had held dear all my life until then. It was slipping out of my fingers, and being replaced with new truth. My tears were also part of the labour pains that accompany any new birth. I was delivered of my ignorance, which is not bliss in the face of truth. I am thankful for the respectful love that led my friend to stay with the argument and not to leave me alone with my fantasy; it made me feel valued. After that I began to enjoy reading different translations alongside my little black Bible. I was able to travel on in the life of faith.

A story like that is a microcosm of other such struggles. Intellectual, social, professional and spiritual issues can be openly discussed and wrestled with. Or they can be put aside in glass cases of antiquity and observed, like inanimate objects, incapable of change or development. It is a way of trying to confine God. We cling to what we know and are often reluctant to offer our knowledge to further scrutiny or daylight so that it can be tested. We sit tight in our separate corners clutching our cherished beliefs of years, afraid of losing them.

In the same way, professional people can cling to their professionalism and elbow out the laity for fear of losing their status. Intellectuals can create a cabal for clever people who look down on less educated human beings as though they were less intelligent, afraid of being shown up in an intellectual argument. There is a spiritual pride which leaves no room for new truth or dialogue, for fear of losing the essence of faith. We can also fall victim to inverted pride, when we lay-people begin to boast of being more human than the professionals we criticise, and when those without a formal education boast of their ignorance.

Fear is at the root of arrogance, and all of us can become captive to it unless we realise that Christianity is more about the use of weakness than the use of power. There is no need to compete. We have been bidden to love. It is a tragedy when that loving has clearly ceased and we see each other as threats instead of friends.

For instance, every other year in Liverpool, people from all the denominations join in a walk on Pentecost Sunday, along Hope Street between our two cathedrals. As we turn the corner by the Anglican Cathedral there is a small band of people who stand on the pavement protesting. Their faces are full of fear and hatred, their voices are harsh and desperate, and their language is abusive. They wave their Bibles with black leather covers and declare that we, and especially our leaders, have betrayed the faith, by entertaining Roman Catholics in our churches and in our joint quest for the truth about God.

Their shouts always touch me as they are reminiscent of my earlier protestations with my friend. Perhaps they had no one to argue with when they were young and now they have isolated themselves in trying to keep to their fundamental belief. They do not want us with our new-fangled beliefs of ecumenism. Our walk only complicates their position.

∞

It has been suggested that the opposite to loving is inertia. I used to hold the view that loving in relationships would come naturally, and that making an effort was false. But I soon realised how naive that was. Resting on our feelings alone is like an anchored boat. We bob up and down according to the weather, facing everywhere but going nowhere. Love involves commitment and hard work which keeps the boat moving forward, and especially in storms.

Spiritual laziness is not the same as genuine uncertainty or doubting. Making an effort in learning and loving is important, even if we fall flat on our faces with embarrassment. It is an opportunity for growth. These moments of embarrassment humble us and bring us back to reality. Sometimes that reality means that those we look up to for guidance are themselves subject to uncertainty.

For example, I remember a most embarrassing

moment in a Scripture lesson at school. I had a friend who was always a little more successful than I. Keen to impress the teacher, who liked us to ask 'intelligent' questions, my friend and I realised we did not understand a particular word. We both raised our hands, hoping we would be asked first. This time I was the favoured one. Glowing with satisfaction I asked, 'Please Miss Walker, what does circumcision mean?' Quite quickly my satisfaction turned to acute embarrassment when I realised that the teacher was not as pleased with my question as I had hoped. She was taken unawares, and gave an unconvincing reply which left me puzzled and anxious. 'It is a small operation that is performed on a male child,' she said. She asked me to see her afterwards so that she could explain more fully. At the time I wished that I had never asked the question. Afterwards I realised it became part of my growing up. The important thing was not to give up asking questions.

So often we are afraid of looking silly, or making fools of ourselves, so we put off asking a question for a long time – sometimes for ever. That reminds me of the time following an operation many years ago. I had discovered prematurely, through the chance remark of a visitor, that I had been operated on for cancer. It had been discovered during the night in an emergency operation for abdominal pain thought to be appendicitis. Recovering from the shock, I was wondering how long I had to live, but did not dare ask. I was afraid of the answer.

The surgeon visited me regularly. He sat in a corner of my room. After chatting for a few minutes, he would snap his fingers and say, 'Next question'. The key question did not emerge for days. Eventually I asked, 'Will I come out of this place alive?' He answered with an 'it depends . . .' kind of answer; it was neither yes nor no.

He told me the truth, that there was a fifty-fifty chance, but that it depended on a combination of factors which included how much I wanted to live. On balance, he thought I would.

I discovered how much I loved life, and realised it would mean putting in some effort to fight for it. I believed in prayer. His answer dispelled my ignorance, and helped me to identify some facts. I was then free to build on the truth as it had been offered to me and to play my part alongside many others to make the most of my life whatever the outcome. Sometimes the truth will be humbling. In the long run it is always liberating.

But life is not always so dramatic. Searching for truth in more ordinary situations need never stop. In everyday conversations, in discussion groups, in family arguments, we can take courage when truth is veiled and tease it out. Good teachers see themselves as learners. Telling the truth to each other as it is revealed, with loving sensitivity, can leave us free to choose what we want to do with it.

Unless we make the effort, we remain ignorant. Ignorance gives rise to prejudice of all kinds. Unless we ride the fears and embarrassments, we give them the upper hand. Making the effort to ask also encourages others. It shows that we do not know everything, and are prepared to be vulnerable. It is a proper way to be humbled. We must never stop asking questions, for the moment we do, we close the door to truth and to life.

But there is an even more positive way. We can enjoy the process of unravelling mysteries together. For this we need time and patience. Most of all we need the will. Like unravelling a tangled ball of wool, or attempting a complicated piece of research, we can tease out the truth about life in the company of other people. We can engage with exploration, struggles and all. But it takes time.

I am fairly impatient and like quick results. I have a coat that I made years ago. I chose a difficult pattern with a reliable name. It was full of unfamiliar problems. But I gave myself time to work them out, and I enjoyed the process. I was so proud of the finished product that although it is almost threadbare now, I cannot throw it away. It hangs in the wardrobe as a reminder of the rewards of staying with a complicated pattern, and of the lessons in dressmaking I learnt on the way. One of the rewards came in having a proper pride in the end-product of my work.

The temptation to give up the struggle of wrestling with doubts and mysteries can be strong, especially when there is no respite due to exhaustion, persistent illness or other pressures. Unless we allow ourselves plenty of time we may lose sight of our goal, and become battle-weary.

Too much questioning and a surfeit of problems can prevent us from reaching any conclusions at all. It can prevent us from being creative and may stop us listening to God and to others. All questions and no answers will relieve us from the responsibility of making commitments. We will leave ourselves no ground on which to stand, and nothing to show for our beliefs. It will be hard to say the creed with any conviction, and our love for one another will be tentative. Our relationships will lack commitment.

There is nothing tentative about Christ and his life. He came to earth, clear about his identity and with a strong sense of mission and purpose. He came to bring hope to those whose lives were difficult. He came to show us how to be loving and committed in our relationships, and to reassure us that we are not alone.

He showed us that life would include pain and confusion, but that it is an exciting adventure not to be missed. He brought Good News to those in need and was angry with religious hypocrites. He pointed to a higher authority and the need to worship. He invited us to follow him.

9
Clinging and Yearning

*Somewhere between the clinging and the yearning
is a place of poise and readiness. Here we can hold
our heads high as we face life or death, with dignity
and humour.*

Clinging to life or clinging to anything implies a note
of desperation and a reluctance to let go. A limpet,
vulnerable and threatened yet fully alive, hangs on to
its rock with ferocious energy when it is touched. Its
energy is channelled into surviving. It may be the same
for us.

For example, whenever we go on holiday, I dread
packing. Over the years I have tried establishing new
routines to take fewer things, but something drives me
to pack for every eventuality. In go clothes for tropical to
arctic conditions. In case I get bored I include my paints,
books, tapestry and games, and pocket radio. To guard
against the need for a doctor a small first aid kit is
tucked in, and to save money, hairdressing equipment.
On occasions we have even found a corner for a bunch
of flowers from a much loved garden which I find hard
to leave behind.

It is a wrench to part with the place that I know and
love for an unknown one, even though travel excites me
and the thought of relaxing, away from day-to-day work
demands, is always attractive. I can yearn for this kind
of respite, yet when it comes near to reality I draw back,
and begin to make provision for my imagined insecurity.

I go into survival overdrive. I can understand why some people prefer not to go on holiday at all because preparing for it is such an effort. But once the wheels are rolling the initial excitement of going away returns.

It was when I stopped to look back on the possible reasons behind this behaviour, that it began to appear more rational. A modest look at the past threw up some interesting facts. By the time I was ten years old our family had moved eight times. Being war-time these moves included evacuation, and I had also a prolonged hospital stay. It was unsettling for all of us. Relationships kept changing as much as the landscape. The constant factor was what we created between us. It was our love for each other and the knowledge that God was there in our comings and goings, and our ups and downs, which helped us. My grandmother used to quote from the Bible, 'Here we have no continuing city, but seek one to come.' This obviously gave her hope, but it did not stop my mother hoping for a settled home for all of us in this life. We shared that hope. Eventually, while my father was away, my mother used her savings to buy a house against strong pressure from her Victorian father.

But it is not just home comforts we cling to. We can also hang on to people and beliefs, as though our life depended on it. This clinging prevents us from being ready to move forward, and from being open to one another in love. It ensures that we live our lives like limpets instead of soaring like birds in the clear air, free to dip and swirl and stretch our wings. But we are neither limpets nor birds, but human beings. We have our freedom now. It is the freedom to choose whether we live, half-live or die.

We need understanding to take our freedom and make a good choice. Nevertheless it is comforting to know that it is all right to be like a limpet for a little longer, if that is what we want to do. We may need to. A friend said to me when I was complaining of my inability to pack more economically, 'What's wrong with that? It is you. I'm just the same. Why change?' I felt she understood. It makes me want to loosen my grip a little more. Her acceptance helped me to accept myself.

There are areas of our lives which frighten us still. It takes time to unclench our fists and to believe that we shall survive with our hands more open. And the more baggage we gather, the more there is to relinquish. So we hang on tighter and it becomes a vicious circle. Not letting go can become burdensome. In time we cannot easily distinguish between the people and things we value most and the rest. So we postpone the sorting out to another day when, we persuade ourselves, there will be more time. For instance we can go on collecting new friends without cherishing the old. We can fight off any suggestion that we may not be in control of our relationships or our possessions.

In reality we know we are not in complete control of our lives and never will be this side of the grave. It is easy to lose sight of the fact that, like every other human being who struggles, we are not unique. Guarding against self-deception is paramount, as we are masters of the art. Finding a way of living more truthfully is a goal worth aiming at. Believing that no one can see us struggling may be what we want to project. Like the man in the parable that Jesus told, who had built bigger and better barns for his hoarded grain at the expense of his soul, we too can deceive ourselves. In the story God calls this man a fool.

∾

Valuing the gift of life is important. Because of my

experience of cancer, I have become deeply thankful for my own life. I know other people who have similarly changed their perspective on living. They have come to see what is really significant. Just before he died I visited a friend who was suffering from cancer. He also treasured his life. He talked about 'the sanctity of the present moment', and spoke with regret of the frantic busyness that he had allowed himself to be caught up with. Now, with time to think, he did not cling to his life, but took firm hold of what was left. He showed gratitude for it. He could see more clearly what was really valuable. He put his energy into each moment, while knowing that death could visit him at any time. Now that his life was being curtailed through illness, he could see more clearly what he had been doing. He could see others caught up in the survival syndrome and it made him sad and indignant at the unnecessary waste.

For some people in the world surviving is their only option. Poverty, famine and war are cruel masters. It is no wonder that people so enslaved cling to their lives. Their lives speak to us daily on our television screens.

But for many of us this is not the only option. We have more choice; we do not have merely to survive. If our energy level is low then there may be something we can do to improve it. It is possible that we have not yet realised the choices open to us. This may be because life has dealt us blows from which we are still reeling: we cannot see anything to look forward to; there is no good news; there is no sense of purpose and nothing to go on living for. We may feel thrown on the scrap heap in the prime of life.

If that is the case, then the thought of making choices in a space between clinging and yearning may feel like a person with agoraphobia who is asked to walk across a large field alone. Even the thought is terrifying. Trying to take steps leads to panic and a feeling of unreality. Seeing others taking the same walk makes you feel even more disabled and helpless. You want to go back to the safety of your own home and close the door. You hope that it is only a nightmare and will be gone in the morning. But it is not a nightmare; it is real. Many people look at life that way and do not know where to turn. That life space seems to stretch on for an eternity.

Having been there, I understand what it is like. One of the secrets is not to fight the fears, but look at them one by one. Another is not to face them alone. Being fearful is human and part of being alive. It is nothing to be ashamed of. Nevertheless shame is something we feel. We want to hide what we are feeling from others in case they do not understand. We cannot face another rejection. We cannot face more pain. Going back to safety is all right in the short term, and it is good to pause. It is a comfort and solace, but staying there for ever is not the way to healing. It is not the way to growth.

Our life space is made up of moments. All of them are in the present. We cannot live ten minutes from now. In the present moment, however miserable, there will be something good to identify and hold to, something to be thankful for – a friendship, a photograph or treasured possession with happy memories, or a talent for something may be among the good things. We can be thankful for being alive. Making a more modest choice about what to do, however difficult it seems, can make a real difference. Making no choice only increases the dithering and prolongs the agony. Instead of standing before the open field of life shaking with insecurity, we can decide to lean on the gate just for the moment. We can tell ourselves the truth of what is happening. We can tell a friend the truth as well. We can tell God.

Feeling trapped we are still free agents. Perhaps we do not have to cross the field at all. Life may lie down another road altogether. Living in the present moment is an art to cultivate. In time the old confidence returns, though not perhaps as we imagined.

∾

It is often helpful to observe small children. Their unaffected behaviour can inspire us to want to do things we never dreamed we could. Their belief in us is a precious gift. It is like when a friend of mine wrote to me about being at a swimming pool with his five-year-old son. 'Daddy,' said the boy, 'Can you jump off the top board?' My friend, who had married later in life and who had never done it before, said it was his son's innocent expectancy that helped him up the ladders which seemed to lead to heaven. It seemed a long way to the water below. He paused, took a deep breath, looked at his expectant son at the side of the pool and jumped. 'He took it all for granted,' he said.

A child may expect and hope for more from us than we expect from ourselves, though it will not always involve jumping from the top board. God made us capable of more than we think. Hope makes all the difference. It helps us to lift up our heads and go for it instead of settling for a life where our heads hang down with despair and hopelessness. There is a place where we can hold our heads high and look forward to something better.

Being fully alive, rather than just surviving or partly living, means that we are channelling our energies creatively, and not simply fending off the more destructive elements of life. We can prepare for death without being depressed by the thought of it or being obsessed by it. In the space between our arriving and departing, we can find a way of life that is more purposeful and positive, and which generates more loving. Somewhere, in that space in between, is a creative tension where our energy is at its height.

Dealing with my agoraphobia taught me to look at my limitations. We need to accept our limitations. This does not mean being resigned to them; it means owning them and then seeing what we can do in the light of that reality. We may be surprised at the doors that begin to open.

Sometimes those limitations make us feel small and foolish, and we put ourselves down. It distresses me to hear expressions like 'I'm no good at anything' or 'I'm useless'. Once, when several of us were discussing hobbies, a woman said, 'I genuinely do not think I have any talents at all.' She was a professional person and spoke as though she was convinced. An awareness of talents, gifts, whatever we call them, gives us the opportunity to be creative and to extend ourselves. Without that extension or expression of life we quietly give up living fully and sink into surviving. We leave being creative to people we call 'arty' or 'academic', believing we have nothing special to offer. In time, if we do not express ourselves through some outlet, our energy dries up and all we look forward to is deliverance from a boring humdrum life where we feel cut off from other people, and eventually to death. Putting ourselves down should never be the end of the story for any human being made in the image of God.

Another pitfall which prevents hope is to be proud of being no good at anything. We can boast about our uselessness. Our fear of failure, or of being thought arrogant, drives us to avoid the truth that we have something to contribute to the wider community, however modest. It absolves us from making an effort. It is like burying our creativity in the ground. It lets us off the demanding side to loving and it keeps people from making demands that frighten us. We are left in peace. But in time that peace becomes a lonely, unfulfilled and stagnant place where we peer out of our barricaded life watching others do their living while we do our existing. To avoid this arid place it helps to sit down with a good companion and start to list the things and people that make us feel really alive. We can begin to redress the balance, perhaps for the first time since childhood. Sometimes another person can be more objective, and can see our talents and gifts better than we can at first. Eventually we need to notice and own them for ourselves. We need to believe in ourselves.

I met a woman like that. She had given up believing in herself. She had given up cleaning her home. She sat depressed and imprisoned, within her four walls, convinced she had nothing to offer. She had been like that for twenty years, since her mother died. After talking together we discovered that she used to be a most creative person, particularly with her needle. She showed me some of her work from the past. Her mother had been a demanding woman, and difficult to please. My friend had married and then had felt driven by the need to be perfect, and it had broken her will to try. She looked surprised and amazed that I had spotted the person inside her who had given up and found that she was still there and fighting to get out. Somehow she had been put on hold.

Several weeks later I visited her again. She had been doing some cleaning. At her feet lay a pile of blue knitting. She was making a jumper for her grown-up daughter. She had never knitted before. The sparkle was back in her eyes. She was living again, and full of hope. A year or two later she volunteered to help with a public charity event in our garden, and loved every minute of it. She has since flown to Ireland to visit her relations after a long gap, and now assists in a centre for elderly people.

∾

Life often arises out of suffering. We can look for light in the darkest places. Hope can spring from despair. Moments of hope, like seeing my friend with the blue knitting, can be discovered in our day-to-day lives. But there is a greater hope that lies beyond this life. We need to lift our eyes to something beyond. That means looking at what we think about death.

Death is the great letting-go. When we are young we do not think about it, unless it is brought to our notice. In old age, it is often in our thoughts. In between youth and old age we have been given the opportunity to prepare for it. But on the whole we prefer to put off talking about it until we have to. It becomes something that happens to someone else. Perhaps we even dream that we can avoid it altogether.

But if we do not think about it during our lifetime until it is forced on us, it comes as an unwelcome shock. Our balance is disturbed. It all depends whether we regard death as a letting-go to something better – or to something worse than life as we know it now. Either way it will be letting go to an unknown. Death is natural. It is inevitable and is something we all must face. It would be better if we were ready.

Death is not something we naturally yearn for, unless we are mortally ill or in pain or despair. But we do yearn for something better. Without that yearning, life does not have much purpose. It becomes something to suffer and endure. The moments of joy and gladness, and of feeling whole, become just moments of respite.

They are a reflection or foretaste of nothing else, unless we see them as trailing something greater beyond this life – a glimpse of heaven.

Christ taught a great deal about the Kingdom of God. The prospect of this new way of life was good news only to those who suffered most and to those who were conscious of their need for forgiveness, for healing and freedom from despair. This place was offered as something we could both experience now through glimpses or hints, and also help to create for the future. For the blind man who received his sight, and for the woman taken in adultery who knew that she was forgiven, the Kingdom of God must have seemed very near.

Sometimes we can provide new hope for those in despair, like the man who was trying to face up to the death of his wife who had been cared for in a hospice. The family care-worker responsible explained to him that she was providing a safe place in which he could express what he was feeling. She told him that there would be no interruptions, and that no one would judge him, and that she was there to help him face his tragedy. She showed him a ready box of tissues should he need them. After a while she realised that the man, who was a shy person by nature, had a lot of pent-up grief and would need more than a tissue or two. So she fetched a clean towel and offered it to him. It was something in which to bury his face should he need to.

As he began to let go some of his feelings, she realised that he needed even more security and personal space, as his face had become contorted and he was embarrassed to be seen like that. Something was blocking the tears from coming. So she gently lifted the towel right over his head and covered it while he was talking, giving him a further measure of privacy. He found that easier and eventually he was able to let go. 'This is bizarre,' he said, but preferred to stay covered for a while. The towel became a face-saver enabling him to retain a measure of personal dignity at a most difficult time.

∾

Those who care for the dying in our hospitals, hospices and homes have much to share with the rest of us. It seems that those who are closest to death have the greatest insight into what life is all about. Here, pretence and pride can be put aside without losing essential human dignity. At the gates of death we are ourselves, like it or not. To know that we are accepted as we are before we depart is surely a glimpse of something better. The hospice movement enables people to be fully themselves to the end. They become known to each other. Those who work there, and those who suffer, face death together. Together they prepare for and work towards something better, without fear.

I received a letter from one worker who said this:

One of the great rewards of our job in hospice work is that we are allowed to *know* people. The veneer which we so carefully apply is discarded, and the loveliness of the real person comes through. Everywhere there is heroism – unsung – unrecognised, until the courage comes to discard the covering, and allow us to marvel at the will to overcome, albeit sometimes only come to terms with great hardship. Then and only then can we share their lives, and in doing so, share our lives with them.

At the point of death all that is false about us falls away and, whatever else we face, we face our essential selves, warts and all. That is a disturbing thought, until I hear once again the voice of the hospice worker. It is possible to know and be known before we die, and also to be loved and accepted. As well as the warts, there is a loveliness too. But we will only be able to do that if we are prepared to be truthful from the inside out, day after day, with ourselves and with those who are close to us. In learning to accept both our warts and our loveliness, God will be there too, reminding us that we are loved and that he will be there after death.

Once we can accept this, we shall be ready. We will not be embarrassed. There will be nothing to fear. We will not need to shelve that conversation about death because we will have nothing to hide. The trouble is we are not always truthful. We hide behind that veneer. We behave as though death was not part of life, which is one of the biggest deceptions of all.

ᔓ

Each day we meet a point of death in miniature which is also a point of life. On the day I was writing this I experienced something which felt dangerous. I felt vulnerable and exposed. David and I were away on retreat. Over breakfast we had agreed to share some of our experience of the previous hour of private reading and prayer. These had been close and special times when we had grown closer in mutual understanding of each other and in our search for God. That morning I had been reading a book which had interested and excited me. I wanted to share some of my gleanings with him.

As soon as I began to speak, I was aware that he was listening intently. I found myself becoming over-anxious to make my points clearly and do myself justice. I had put David on a professional pedestal. I knew his grasp of the Bible text was superior to mine. It had been part of his training. A small voice on my shoulder

whispered, 'You'd better get it right. If you don't you'll
be clobbered, and down you will go.'

'Getting it right' meant being theologically correct.
The book had stretched me intellectually and I was
enjoying the challenge of swimming out of my depth.
Talking about it and being listened to, made me realise
that I was rapidly climbing a self-made pedestal. It was
called 'Theologian, or Intelligent Layperson whose
knowledge of God is as valid as any clergyperson's,
especially a man's'.

David's questions were persistent and penetrating.
Instead of acknowledging ignorance at certain points, I
stuck to my guns and struggled on, trying to do justice
to the author as well as provide the perfectly framed
answer. I found myself in some kind of competition.
A conversation between loving equals had become the
beginnings of a battle. I not only wanted to share in an
intellectual conversation with my husband, I found
myself wanting to prove something without losing face
in the attempt. The very intellectual stimulation that I
usually enjoy turned into a conflict where my ammu-
nition was running low. My pride would not allow me
to say, 'I don't know'. I was afraid of showing my ignorance, without realising that it was already evident.

While listening intently, David began to discuss and
question some of the points I had raised, as an equal.
Inside, I tumbled off my pedestal to the ground. The
account of what had originally excited me became less
succinct under the clear gaze of an interested listener
until I felt my self-esteem falling. I was tempted to give
up the conversation altogether and walk away.

In fact I was tumbling from my self-made pedestal
to the ground of my own ordinariness, which felt like
worthlessness. That made me compete even with my
own husband. It felt as though questions were coming

from an adversary rather than from a husband and friend. And that felt like approaching miniature deaths: the death of my self-esteem, the death of an ability to enjoy robust conversation on serious topics, and the death of our mutual respect.

We resolved this conflict by stopping it in time, noticing what had happened, being truthful and by knowing that underlying it all there was mutual love and respect. We also saw the funny side. God was there. I acknowledged my resentment and indignation at not being taken seriously in the distant past when wanting to enter into conversations with clergy which involved faith and theology, as though I had little to offer. I acknowledged to myself that it was unrealistic and arrogant to think that I could argue as a professional equal. David acknowledged that while realising my struggles, he did not want to patronise me by changing his tack and softening his approach. So he held nothing back. He insisted that he was treating me as an equal person.

It was after this exchange and after writing an account of it a little more fully that I finally came to earth. I realised that my general resentment and hurt at being excluded from such conversations in the past had a deeper root, which was to do with having been part of a large clergy family. I had to die a little in order to rise again. I had to accept my ordinariness instead of straining to make a good impression. It explained why, for example, I can become preachy at times. There was no need to compete any more; I know I still have something to offer as a Christian woman. It has not dulled my motivation to learn through reading and reasoned argument, but it is ludicrous to think that I could be like a professional theologian without being willing to study and train. It is humbling to make these discoveries, but also liberating. It clears the way for new life to flow more freely. It is like coming upon a clearing, after trudging through the forest. We arrive at a place of energy and greater understanding.

Next time I enter into an intellectual argument I shall be able to smile a little at the memory of my downfall on that occasion, and shall argue only from ground that is truly mine. It is good to know that I am all right as I am, without the frills – known and accepted and loved. That is good news; it is also a relief. In the end it is not impressions that matter but the genuine article.

Our yearning for something better is natural and necessary. But holding fast to that which is good and true about ourselves, about each other and about God now, will help us to let go willingly of all that is false, before we are forced to at the end of our lives. It will also also prevent cynicism and apathy poisoning the system. Looking forward to the complete experience of how God dreamed the world to be, is incentive enough to live now. But the possibility of bringing his Kingdom forward is always there for us to turn into a present reality. Without vision, we are told in the Bible, people perish.

Somewhere in the space between the clinging and the yearning we can find a place of poise and readiness. There, with our heads held high, we can face life or death with dignity and humour. We can do that together, provided we remember that God loves us, and that we are prepared to be honest and loving with ourselves now, in the light of that truth. We shall be limpets no longer, nor even birds. We shall be fully alive, interdependent human beings, who are learning to follow the commandments to love God and our neighbours as ourselves, putting in some effort, and hopefully with a little more humility.

10
Coming Home

We arrive at a place where we are known and loved and from where we continue our journeying: with God and to God, and with one another. It is a place of living and worship.

After journeying it is good to come home. Like an animal we can go to ground. We can relax and be ourselves. It is even better if there is someone we love waiting for us with the kettle on and the lights burning.

This journey would not be complete without a reminder of the destination. Although we began with questions about the real meaning of humility, we will have reached our destination if we have acquired a greater understanding and a sharper personal awareness of our identity and that of our neighbour. Not only that, for if we have penetrated the mystery of God a little more, we will be better equipped to answer the underlying question of this search which has been 'Is it all right to love myself? And how do I do that without becoming arrogant and selfish?'

The important thing is that we are more alive than when we started, and hopefully more loving. For we have travelled in the company of the God of love.

It has become obvious that this has been a journey within a journey, because these are questions that remain with us all our lives. But it has been illuminating to focus on them in this way. It has been challenging to answer them as truthfully as possible. Although we have dared to face some extremes, much of the time has been spent treading the ground of our ordinariness; that space between the pits and the pedestals of life.

Several things stand out for me. First, there is the importance of understanding the word 'respect'; secondly, the place of stigma, or marks of disgrace, and how to live with them; and thirdly, the concept of faithfulness. These naturally progress for me to the need to worship which involves looking again and again at what we value and then valuing it, being honest, and saying 'thank you'.

Respect means 'to look again'. Taking a second look is a safeguard against hasty ill-informed judgement and prejudice. It acts as a buffer.

Antony Gormley, the sculptor, has provided a different way of taking this second look. In his work, 'Field for the British Isles', thousands of terracotta figurines were formed individually by people from a local community, working in collaboration with the sculptor. A photographic detail of the work appears on the cover of this book. Each person was given a handful of clay, and asked to form a figure twelve inches high, with no arms or legs, and eye holes made with a finger. These figures were collected, fired and placed shoulder to shoulder on the floor filling a bare room in a selected Art Gallery.

I saw the exhibit in Liverpool's Tate Gallery. In confronting such 'a field full of people' I was confronted myself. Here was no hostile crowd. Their upturned faces held me with their gaze. They left me with questions. Who do you think we are? Who are you? What are you going to do now? There was an air of expectancy. I could not be apathetic. Something deep in me stirred in response. Somehow my answers were crucial to the nature of my relationship with them. 'They' became

'us'. We had begun a conversation. I was reminded of
my friends in the South African encounter described at
the beginning of this book.

Respecting God means we give him another chance
to get through to us. It gives us more opportunity to
probe his nature. Respecting others gives them room
to be themselves before we rush to label them for our
convenience. Respecting myself prevents me from either
putting myself down in a pit of self-deprecation which
is unfitting for someone made in God's image, or setting
myself up on a pedestal of self-importance to be what I
am not. It means being kind to one another and to
ourselves. Respect is a step towards grace and love and
is something we can both give and receive. It leaves
room for forgiveness. This threefold thread of mutual
esteem between God, others and self is once again
dependent on how honest and responsive we are able
and willing to be. Humility is facing reality.

One of the challenges that I have been compelled to
face is about living with stigma. Throughout this journey I have become more aware of my own vulnerability.
I have become more sensitive to the times when my
pride is hurt, and when I have been tempted to justify
myself, or to put the record straight. Equally my awareness of God and his acceptance has been heightened. I
have had to learn to take resting places on the journey,
and to say 'yes' and 'no' to things and people more
appropriately, and to give myself more space. I have also
tried to give more space to others. I have drawn strength
from looking away from myself towards the one who
spoke to his Father from the cross at a time of public
disgrace.

At times I have had to face some facts which I had
hoped would disappear into history. One of those facts
is the stigma attached to having had a breakdown or

having lived with a phobia. It is greater than the one attached to having had cancer. Having been in both those dark places many years ago, it has been easier to talk about the latter. There is a kind of glory attached to surviving cancer, but a breakdown is still not 'respectable'. It leaves a person's reputation tarnished in a way that leads some to doubt whether he or she is capable of taking real responsibility again. A marked health record affects job prospects, and it can damage a person's social life and relationships while he or she works to regain self-confidence and raise a lowered self-esteem. It is no wonder that people prefer to keep these things quiet. But I believe we must not, for two reasons.

The first reason is to fend off self-deception and fantasy. The second is to bring release. Without allowing others into our lives a little more, we deprive one another of a truth about being human that can liberate and energise. Talking about these things reduces ignorance and helps us to be more human and sincere, and does not necessarily make us more neurotic. We find that we are not pretending or alone, and this enables us to hold up our heads and to look our neighbours in the eye, knowing that they too may well be struggling with something that makes them feel ashamed or diminished, somewhere in their lives. Once, after I had given a talk, someone in the audience stood up to suggest that it was good for me to have written about these things. 'Yes,' I said, 'it was.' Feeling patronised, I couldn't resist adding, 'and I hope it has been good for you as well.' He had the grace to tell me afterwards that it had been.

People do get better from mental illness, just as they do from physical illness. But there are other forms of stigma from which there is often no relief. Having a past prison sentence, being involved in a court case, or in a false accusation of abuse; being HIV or having

AIDS, being unemployed, elderly or disabled; being a lone parent or black, being poor, or a woman; all carry their own stigma in our society. Respecting – that is, taking another look at – the people behind the labels, we will often find wisdom, courage, talent and interesting articulate personalities which make nonsense of the current attitudes which stigmatise such people and make them feel rejected and counted worthless in our society. No wonder there is sometimes indignant protest. It is a righteous anger, a cry for dignity and for justice.

Living in a city like Liverpool for nearly twenty years and being aware of unbalanced reporting based on prejudice and past wounds makes me indignant too. Liverpool has had an image problem and, while this is changing markedly, it takes time to live down certain shameful facts in the city's history. It takes a good deal of self-confidence and knowledge to remember the glorious facts as well, and stand still while others throw the stones.

Visiting reporters tend to see what they want to see or what they have been instructed to look for. In an elegant waterfront city they see only the riot-torn streets and, overlooking the hardworking and successful people – many of whom are involved in voluntary work in their spare time – they see only criminality and unemployment, both of which are features of any modern big city. What they miss is the insight and resilience of the people who have been hurt and who know how to care for one another. They miss the stories of those who have been around longer and who are part of present history in the making. Liverpool people have a flair for living.

Owning the history can make us feel both proud and ashamed of ourselves at the same time. It can also save us from getting onto our high horse too often. Willy

Russell, the Liverpool playwright, who lives in our village of Woolton, captured the truth of owning ourselves, warts and all, in the words put into the mouth of his character, Shirley Valentine, a Liverpool housewife.

'I've come to like myself – really,' I said to him, I said. 'I think I'm alright Joe. I think that if – if I saw me, I'd say that woman's OK, she's alive. She's not remarkable, she's not gonna – gonna be there in the history books. But she's there in the time she's livin' in. An' certainly she's got her wounds . . . and her battle scars, but maybe a little bit of the bullshit is true – an' the wounds shouldn't be hidden away . . . because – because even the wounds and the scars are about being alive.'*

Knowing myself accepted and loved, marks and all, without having to be perfect first, is of the essence of my faith. A God who accepts me like that stimulates my will to live, both for him and for others, and to respect myself. Believing in a God like that increases my awareness of my shortcomings and, I hope, my understanding of the shortcomings of others, without leaving them or me feeling driven into a corner from which there is no escape. Forgiveness then makes sense. I am driven to worship, which includes looking at Christ again and again.

If we look again at the way Christ regarded his own wounds, his stigmata, we find that he did not hide them. He said to Thomas, the doubting disciple, as he showed him the nail prints, 'Look at my hands and my feet,' and, where the spear entered, 'Put your hand into my side.' It was an invitation to become intimately involved. Was Christ flaunting the signs of his vulnerability, or was he suggesting to Thomas that there was something significant about them that he needed to know? Was he

*From the script of William Russell's play, *Shirley Valentine*.

perhaps wanting Thomas to be doubly sure that God became human and was hurt like the rest of us, and that that was not the end, but only part of the story: that there is life after death?

Respecting the wounds of Christ and the forgiveness of which they speak, helps us to face our own wounds. He has been called 'the Wounded Healer'. We can follow him in lesser ways and bring life to others by taking the risk of being a little more open than is conventional or comfortable, and by accepting the woundedness of others. We will gain more than we lose.

People frequently say to me, with an anxious caring look in their eyes, 'How are you nowadays?', and my response has tended to be a bristling, 'Thank you, but what do you mean, *nowadays*?', wishing that they would not remind me of past problems. I am, however, learning to relax and, I trust, to be more gracious too. Without wishing to sound too pious, I am thankful to be rescued from the precarious existence of taking up residence on a pedestal of perfection. I am thankful to be noticed at all, and recognise that, even if *I* know that nearly forty years have passed since the breakdown, and nearly thirty since having cancer, others have not been counting. To some it may seem like yesterday. Indeed they may not be interested or anxious about me at all, they may be anxious for themselves and looking for hope.

I have become aware that it is no good hoping that we can stuff certain facts of our history away in a cupboard, as though they were old clothes and had nothing to do with us any more. They have a habit of re-emerging, either in our dreams and nightmares or in reality sooner or later. Living with a stigma, or even a skeleton in the cupboard, is something that many people face privately, and prefer not to talk about. But that means living in fear of disclosure, which can cause us to be unsociable and withdrawn – like an elderly friend who was living in a retirement home. She was reluctant to join the others at meal times, in case it came to light that she had been admitted to a mental hospital when she was a young woman. She preferred to stay in her room. In fact she was gifted with a wry sense of humour which was appreciated by those of us who visited and cared for her.

These things which threaten our dignity do not have to be shouted from the house tops on every occasion, but it is better if they are owned, and expressed somehow, maybe through poetry, painting, prose, prayer or in ordinary conversation with a friend. This is a way to self-respect and an antidote to self-doubt. It will help us to understand and respect our neighbour as we respect ourselves, and will be another step towards loving our neighbour as ourselves, as we have been commanded. It is a step nearer home, the place where we are known and loved, and from where we continue our journeying; with God, and to God and with one another.

Throughout my journey I have also been aware of the place of faithfulness. Keeping faith ensures that we stay connected; breaking faith affects relationship. Preserving the relationship with God, with others and with ourselves is vital for loving to be effective. I am thankful for those who have believed in me. They encouraged me when setting out and have stuck by me throughout. I have also had to believe in myself. Above all, God has been there keeping me in touch and reminding me of his love through so many aspects of his creation, till sometimes I have felt overwhelmed. My responsibility has been to know what I wanted to do, and then to believe and to go on believing, even when the mist came down and the signposts were unclear. I have had to stay alive to his faithful love.

Staying alive like this depends, like light and power, on there being a reliable source and an uninterrupted circuit. Nowadays there are overriding arrangements for many of the temporary breaks that occur. For instance, one day when water penetrated my iron, the power on that circuit was cut off. A switch indicates OFF when that happens, and I can then turn it on again. This overrides the fault and restores power to the neighbouring machines that have been affected. I can make sure that it does not happen again by taking another look at the iron, as it may need attention.

In the Trinity – God the Father, the Son and the Holy Spirit – I see an unbroken and continuous relationship where love flows unchecked for ever. We have been invited to participate in this relationship. We belong to one another and can give and receive life and love, especially when there are breaks and faults. God's faithfulness is constant. He gives us time and opportunity to rectify our faults and betrayals and to repair the breaks, through one another. His forgiveness and understanding overrides. He is there to ensure that life goes on, so that we can stand up and start again.

That makes me want to worship him. It enables me to get things into perspective. Then, aware of his grace, I can lift my head with proper pride and say, 'thank you'. With my feet firmly planted on the ground, I am ready to face another day.

Further Reading

Peter Clare, *The Stations of the Cross* (a book of woodcuts). Redlake Press 1994.

Ruth Etchells, *Just As I Am: Personal Prayer for Every Day*. SPCK 1994.

Antony Gormley (an exhibition catalogue with narrative). Tate Gallery 1994.

Brian Keenan, *An Evil Cradling*. Hutchinson 1992.

Sister Margaret Magdalen CSMV, *The Hidden Face of Jesus*. Darton, Longman and Todd 1993.

Tony Parker, *Life After Life*. New edn., HarperCollins 1995.

M. Scott Peck, *A World Waiting to be Born*. Rider 1994.

Brian Thorne, *Behold the Man*. Darton, Longman and Todd 1991.

Carlos Valles, *Let Go of Fear*. Triumph 1991.

Harry Williams, *The True Wilderness*. New edn., Mowbray 1994.

Psalms 8, 25, 27, 34, 40, 103, 130, 131, 139.